Ctrl+Alt+Lead

KARI-ANN LEIGHTON

Dedication

To all the leaders who are brave enough to embrace change, to those who inspire others to think differently, and to those who lead with passion and purpose, may this book empower you to navigate the digital jungle confidently and positively impact the world, knowing that your leadership can make a significant difference. Embracing change is not just about adapting, it's about seizing the opportunity to empower yourself and your team.

Preface

In the ever-evolving digital jungle, a metaphor for the complex and rapidly changing digital business environment, the art of leadership is being redefined. The days of rigid command-and-control models are fading, replaced by a new era of agility, innovation, and emotional intelligence. This book is your compass in this exciting but complex terrain.

We'll explore the key principles of modern leadership, examining how to cultivate strong teams, navigate the complexities of remote work, and foster a culture of creativity and resilience. Through real-world examples, insights from industry leaders, and a healthy dose of humor, you'll gain the tools and mindset to thrive in the 21st century.

Whether you're a seasoned CEO or just starting your leadership journey, this book is your guide to success in the digital jungle. Prepare to embrace the power of technology, human connection, and a forward-thinking approach. **It's time to Ctrl+Alt+Lead!**

Introduction

The world is moving faster than ever. Technology is disrupting industries, information is shared at lightning speed, and the traditional rules of business are being rewritten. In this whirlwind of change, leading effectively is more crucial than ever.

But leadership in the digital age is a far cry from the command-and-control models of the past. The old ways of barking orders and demanding obedience need to be updated.

Today's successful leaders can inspire, motivate, and empower their teams in a dynamic and ever-changing environment.

This book is your journey into the heart of modern leadership. We'll explore the key principles that drive success in the digital world, offering practical advice and thought-provoking insights to help you become a leader who can adapt, innovate, and make a lasting impact.

Get ready to challenge your assumptions, expand your leadership toolbox, and unlock your potential as a leader who can confidently navigate the digital jungle and create a brighter future for your team and your organization.

Contents

Chapter 1

Rethinking Leadership

The Digital Age Shift

The digital revolution has swept through every facet of our lives, transforming how we work, communicate, and think. This transformative wave has also profoundly reshaped the landscape of leadership. Gone are the days of the lone, charismatic figure at the helm, barking orders from a gilded office. Leadership is a dynamic, collaborative, and often virtual dance in the digital age.

Imagine a world where information flows freely, ideas are instantly shared across continents, and a constant feedback loop fuels innovation. This is the reality for leaders in the 21st century. To navigate this ever-changing landscape, leaders must shed their old paradigms and embrace new thinking. They must be agile, adaptable, and empathetic. They must be able to connect with their teams, inspire them, and empower them to be their best.

The rise of digital tools and platforms has revolutionized the way we work. Teams are no longer confined to physical office spaces. Instead, they are scattered across the globe, connected by virtual threads of communication and collaboration. This shift has created a new set of challenges and opportunities for leaders. They must foster trust and accountability in a virtual environment, build a cohesive team culture despite physical distance, and ensure clear and effective communication.

Think of it this way: In the past, leadership was often about maintaining control and imposing directives. But in the digital age, leadership is about creating a shared vision, fostering a culture of collaboration, and empowering individuals to take ownership of their work. It's about leading with empathy, understanding the needs of your team, and being a source of support and guidance rather than simply issuing commands. As a leader, you play a crucial role in fostering this culture of collaboration and trust.

The digital age has also ushered in a new era of innovation.

Technology constantly evolves, and companies must adapt quickly to stay ahead. This requires leaders to be forward-thinking, embrace change, and cultivate a culture of experimentation. It means encouraging employees to think outside the box, challenge the status quo, and bring new ideas to the table.

Imagine a leader stuck in the past, clinging to outdated methods and resisting change. This leader would likely find themselves quickly outmatched by the rapid pace of innovation in the digital age. Conversely, a leader who embraces change is curious, adaptable, and willing to experiment and learn will thrive in this dynamic environment.

However, adaptability and innovation are not enough. Leaders in the digital age must also possess a deep understanding of human behavior and the ability to build strong relationships.

This is where emotional intelligence comes into play. It is the ability to understand and manage one's emotions and those of others. It is the ability to empathize with your team, listen actively, and communicate effectively, even when things get tough. Understanding the importance of emotional intelligence in leadership can enlighten you and make you more aware of its significance in the digital age.

Consider a brilliant leader who lacks emotional intelligence. They may be able to come up with great ideas, but they might need help motivating their team or building strong relationships. This can lead to frustration, disengagement, and, ultimately, a decrease in productivity. On the other hand, a leader who is highly emotionally intelligent can build trust and loyalty, inspire their team, and create a positive and productive work environment.

The digital age is not just about technology. It is also about people. It's about understanding the unique needs and motivations of each individual on your team and creating a culture where everyone feels valued, heard, and empowered.

It's about fostering a sense of community and belonging, even when your team is spread across the globe.

In the end, effective leadership in the digital age is about something other than being the most intelligent person in the room or having the most technical expertise. It's about being a leader who understands the needs of their team, who can inspire them to achieve great things, and who can guide them through the complexities of the digital landscape. It's about being a human, empathetic leader committed to building a better future for the team and the organization.

As we continue to navigate the ever-changing digital age, the need for effective leadership has never been greater. By embracing the principles outlined in this book, leaders can equip themselves with the skills and mindset to thrive in this dynamic environment. It's time to ditch the old ways and **Ctrl+Alt+Lead your team to victory!**

Beyond Command and Control

Imagine a world where the traditional command-and-control leadership style thrives on top-down directives and rigid structures and feels as outdated as a rotary phone.

That's the reality of the digital age. The rapid pace of technological change, the rise of remote workforces, and the demand for innovation have thrown the traditional leadership playbook into disarray.

Gone are the days when leaders could dictate orders and expect their teams to follow blindly. Today's successful leaders embrace a more collaborative, agile, and human-centric approach. They empower their teams, foster creativity, and adapt to the ever-changing landscape of the digital jungle.

The limitations of traditional leadership models become glaringly apparent in the digital age. In the past, a top-down approach sufficed. Leaders could rely on their expertise, make decisions unilaterally, and expect their teams to execute without question. However, the rapid evolution of technology, the increasing interconnectedness of global markets, and the rise of diverse, multigenerational workforces have shattered the old paradigms.

Here's why the command-and-control model falls short in the modern workplace:

Lack of Flexibility and Adaptability: The traditional command-and-control approach often needs help to keep pace with the rapid changes in the digital landscape. Rigid structures and top-down decision-making can hinder agility, making responding quickly to new challenges and opportunities easier. Leaders who cling to outdated methods risk being left behind in a world where innovation is paramount.

Stifled Innovation and Creativity: Command-and-control leadership can inadvertently stifle creativity and innovation by creating an environment where employees feel hesitant to express their ideas or take risks. In a culture where decision-making is centralized, employees may be discouraged from thinking outside the box or challenging the status quo. A rigid hierarchy can limit the flow of diverse perspectives and ideas, hindering progress and ultimately hindering growth.

Erosion of Trust and Engagement: When employees are treated as mere cogs in a machine, their engagement and motivation inevitably suffer. The command-and-control model can lead to a lack of trust and disenfranchisement among team members. Employees may feel disconnected from the overall vision and goals, resulting in low morale, reduced productivity, and increased turnover.

Limited Collaboration and Communication: The command-and-control approach often fails to foster effective collaboration and communication. Information silos can form, impeding the free flow of ideas and knowledge. The lack of open dialogue and shared decision-making can lead to misunderstandings, inefficiency, and missed opportunities.

The digital age demands a new breed of leader who is more than just a commander but a true facilitator and catalyst for growth. This new breed understands leadership is not about dictating but inspiring, empowering, and guiding. It's about fostering a culture of collaboration, creativity, and continuous learning.

Instead of barking orders, today's leaders ask questions, listen intently, and seek team input. They build trust and empower their employees to take ownership of their work. They are embracing the power of technology to connect with their teams, no matter where they are in the world.

Take the example of Elon Musk at Tesla. His leadership style is a fascinating case study of balancing innovation with execution in a fast-paced, tech-driven environment. He challenges the status quo, pushes boundaries, and sets audacious goals. However, he also actively listens to his team, embraces their ideas, and provides the resources and support they need to succeed. This blend of vision, ambition, and empowerment is key to Tesla's success.

Consider the shift towards remote work, another transformative force in the digital age. Companies like Netflix, Spotify, and GitLab have embraced remote work models, proving that high-performing teams can thrive, even when geographically dispersed. The success of these companies is a testament to the fact that remote work can be highly productive and engaging, provided that leaders adapt their approaches. Effective communication, trust-building, and a focus on building a strong team culture are essential for successful remote teams.

These examples highlight the critical need for leaders to move beyond the limitations of traditional leadership models. The digital age demands a new leadership paradigm characterized by flexibility, agility, and a deep understanding of human motivation and behavior.

This shift in leadership thinking is about more than embracing new technologies. It's about understanding the fundamental changes in how work is done and the evolving expectations of employees. Leaders must be adept at navigating complex digital ecosystems, embracing new ways of collaborating and fostering a culture that thrives on continuous innovation.

The shift towards a more human-centric approach is crucial.

The digital age is not just about technology; it's about people. Leaders who can connect emotionally with their teams, fostering trust, engagement, and a sense of belonging, will thrive in the digital jungle.

Embracing Change and Innovation

In this ever-changing, technology-driven world, leadership is no longer about issuing commands and dictating every move. It's about adaptability, embracing change, and leading with a forward-thinking mindset. Imagine a captain steering a ship through turbulent waters. The captain doesn't simply shout orders; they constantly analyze the situation, adjust the course, and empower the crew to navigate the challenges. That's what modern leadership is all about.

Think of Elon Musk at Tesla. He's not afraid to push boundaries, embrace bold ideas, and make radical changes. He's a visionary who constantly strives for innovation and disrupts established norms. He's a prime example of a leader who thrives on change, not fearing it but using it as an opportunity to grow and innovate.

Imagine a company stuck in the past, clinging to outdated processes and resisting new technologies. This is a recipe for stagnation and eventual decline. In today's world, businesses that adapt are kept from being left behind. Leaders must embrace innovation, encourage experimentation, and create a culture of welcoming and nurturing new ideas.

Charles Darwin once said, "It's not the strongest of the species that survives, nor the most intelligent, but the one most adaptable to change?" This applies perfectly to leadership in the digital age. Leaders need to be agile, flexible, and open to new ideas. They must be comfortable with ambiguity and uncertainty and inspire their teams to adapt and thrive in a constantly evolving landscape.

Think about the impact of artificial intelligence (AI) on businesses. AI is automating tasks, creating new possibilities, and even impacting the way we work. Leaders need to embrace AI, not fear it. They need to understand how AI can be leveraged to improve efficiency, enhance customer experiences, and unlock new opportunities. By embracing AI and other technological advancements, leaders can drive growth and stay ahead of the curve.

But adaptability doesn't mean abandoning your core values or throwing caution to the wind. It's about balancing embracing change and maintaining a solid foundation. It's about adapting your strategies and approaches while staying true to your company's mission and vision. Think of it like a tree that bends in the wind. It's flexible enough to withstand the storm yet strong enough to stay grounded.

Consider how Netflix has embraced remote work. The company recognized that talented professionals can be free of a physical office today. By embracing remote work, Netflix has created a global team, allowing them to access a wider talent pool and adapt to changing workforce needs. Their focus on communication and collaboration through technology has ensured that team members, no matter where they are, remain connected and productive.

Embracing change and innovation isn't just about technology or work practices; it's also about fostering a culture of continuous learning. Leaders must be lifelong learners and encourage their teams to embrace growth and development. In the rapidly changing world, staying stagnant is a recipe for failure. It's about developing a growth mindset, where setbacks are seen as opportunities for learning and improvement.

Imagine a company that invests heavily in training and development for its employees. They encourage experimentation, provide opportunities for employees to share their ideas, and celebrate learning and growth. This culture of learning creates a dynamic and innovative workforce that is always ready to adapt and thrive.

Embrace change and innovation, and you will unlock a world of possibilities. Be adaptable, embrace new ideas, and encourage your team to do the same. You'll be amazed at what you can achieve when you embrace the challenges and opportunities of the digital age.

The Role of Emotional Intelligence

Imagine walking into a bustling marketplace filled with vendors from diverse backgrounds, each offering unique products and services. To navigate this vibrant marketplace effectively, you need a keen understanding of each vendor's language, cultural nuances, and motivations. This is precisely what effective leadership in today's diverse workplaces requires. Emotional intelligence – the ability to understand and manage your own emotions and those of others – is the currency that allows you to build strong relationships, foster collaboration, and inspire your team to achieve extraordinary things.

With its fast-paced communication and global reach, the digital age requires emotional intelligence like never before. Leading a team of individuals with diverse backgrounds, perspectives, and working styles requires more than just technical skills. It demands empathy, active listening, and thoughtful responses to each team member's needs.

Empathy: The Foundation of Connection

Let's delve into a scenario that illustrates the power of empathy in leadership. Imagine a team working on a complex project, facing tight deadlines and mounting pressure. One member, Sarah, seems withdrawn and less engaged than usual. A leader with high emotional intelligence would recognize that something might be affecting Sarah. Instead of pushing for results, they would approach Sarah empathetically, asking, "Sarah, I noticed you've been quieter than usual. Is everything alright?"

This simple gesture of concern can go a long way in building trust and open communication. It allows Sarah to feel understood and supported, potentially revealing a personal issue impacting her work. By understanding Sarah's situation, the leader can adapt their approach, providing appropriate support and ensuring she feels valued and part of the team.

Active Listening: The Art of Hearing Beyond Words

Active listening goes beyond simply hearing what someone says. It involves engaging with the speaker's emotions, paying attention to their body language, and asking clarifying questions to ensure you fully comprehend their message. In a diverse team, where communication styles can vary greatly, active listening is essential for preventing misunderstandings and fostering a culture of respect.

Consider a team meeting where members are discussing a new strategy. One team member, John, expresses his concerns about the potential impact on a specific client. A leader with strong emotional intelligence would listen attentively, paying attention to John's tone and body language. They might ask, "John, I understand your concerns about the client. Can you elaborate on why you think this strategy might be problematic?" By actively listening and seeking clarification, the leader demonstrates respect for John's perspective, builds trust, and creates an environment where everyone feels heard.

Managing Emotions: Navigating the Rollercoaster

Leading in today's volatile business landscape often means navigating a rollercoaster of emotions. You'll encounter stressful situations, unexpected challenges, and even setbacks. Leaders with high emotional intelligence are skilled at managing their emotions and influencing the team's emotional climate.

Imagine a project facing a significant setback. A leader with low emotional intelligence might react with frustration or anger, causing panic and undermining team morale. A leader with high emotional intelligence would remain calm, acknowledge the setback, and focus on finding solutions.

They might say, "This is a tough situation, but we've overcome challenges before. Let's focus on what we can control and work together to find a way forward." This approach helps to maintain composure, inspire confidence, and guide the team towards a positive outcome.

Developing Emotional Intelligence: A Lifelong Journey

Emotional intelligence is not a static trait; it's a skill that can be cultivated and honed over time. Here are some practical steps for enhancing your emotional intelligence:

Self-Awareness: Become more attuned to your emotions and how they influence your behavior. Practice introspection, journaling, and seeking feedback from trusted colleagues.

Empathy Training: Actively listen to others, seek to understand their perspectives, and practice putting yourself in their shoes. Attend workshops, read books, and engage in activities that promote empathy.

Emotional Regulation: Learn techniques to manage your stress and emotions in challenging situations. Practice mindfulness, deep breathing exercises, and other stress-reduction strategies.

Social Skills Development: Enhance your communication skills, build rapport with others, and practice active listening. Attend networking events, join social groups, and seek opportunities to interact with diverse individuals.

The Transformative Power of Emotional Intelligence

Emotional intelligence is not just a leadership buzzword; it's the key to creating a positive, productive, and inclusive work environment. By embracing empathy, active listening, and emotional regulation, leaders can inspire trust, build strong relationships, and empower their teams to reach their full potential. In the digital age, where change is constant and connection is paramount, emotional intelligence is essential for success.

Cultivating a Growth Mindset

In the modern business landscape, success hinges on adaptability and a relentless pursuit of improvement. Leaders who embrace a growth mindset—a belief that abilities and intelligence can be developed through dedication and effort—are better equipped to navigate the complexities of the digital age. A growth mindset fosters a culture of continuous learning, where challenges are seen as opportunities for growth, and feedback is valued as a catalyst for progress.

Imagine a company where employees are encouraged to explore new ideas, experiment with different approaches, and embrace failure as a stepping stone to success. This is the essence of a growth mindset in action. It's a shift away from the fixed mindset, which views abilities as predetermined and avoids challenges for fear of exposing weaknesses.

Cultivating a growth mindset within an organization requires a deliberate and ongoing effort from leaders. It's not simply about adopting a new philosophy; it's about creating a culture that permeates every aspect of the company. Here are some key strategies for nurturing this mindset:

1 - Embrace a Culture of Continuous Learning:

Invest in Professional Development: Provide employees with access to training programs, workshops, and conferences to expand their skills and knowledge. Please encourage them to pursue certifications, degrees, or other credentials that demonstrate their commitment to growth.

Promote Knowledge Sharing: Create platforms for employees to share their expertise, insights, and best practices. This could be through internal blogs, knowledge repositories, or dedicated mentorship programs.

Foster a Culture of Experimentation: Encourage employees to experiment with new ideas, technologies, and approaches. Celebrate failures as learning opportunities and provide constructive feedback to help them iterate and improve.

Reward Curiosity and Innovation: Recognize and reward employees who demonstrate a passion for learning, actively seek out new knowledge, and are willing to challenge the status quo.

2 - Emphasize Feedback and Development:

Establish a Culture of Open Communication: Encourage open and honest feedback, both positive and constructive.

Create a safe space where employees feel comfortable sharing their thoughts and suggestions without fear of retribution.

Implement Regular Performance Reviews: Use performance reviews to assess performance and provide personalized feedback and development plans.

Focus on identifying areas for improvement and creating a roadmap for growth.

Provide Mentorship and Coaching: Pair employees with experienced mentors or coaches who can guide them through challenges, provide support, and help them develop their skills.

Create Opportunities for Growth: Offer career advancement opportunities, cross-functional projects, or leadership development programs to incentivize employees to continue learning and growing.

3 - Lead by Example:

Model a Growth Mindset: As a leader, you are your organization's most influential role model. Demonstrate your commitment to lifelong learning by actively pursuing new knowledge, seeking feedback, and embracing challenges.

Celebrate Learning and Growth: Recognize and acknowledge employees seeking growth opportunities. Highlight examples of individuals who have overcome challenges and made significant progress in their development.

Encourage Curiosity and Exploration: Foster a sense of curiosity and exploration by asking thought-provoking questions, challenging assumptions, and encouraging employees to think outside the box.

4 - Embrace Technology for Learning and Development:

Utilize Online Learning Platforms: Leverage online learning platforms and resources to provide employees access to various courses, tutorials, and interactive learning experiences.

Leverage AI-powered Tools: Explore using AI-powered tools to personalize learning paths, track progress, and provide personalized feedback.

Promote Gamification: Gamify learning experiences to make them more engaging and enjoyable for employees. This can be through interactive quizzes, simulations, and virtual rewards.

Examples of Growth Mindset in Action:

Netflix: Netflix has a strong culture of experimentation and learning. The company encourages employees to try new ideas and take risks, and they learn from their failures. They have a culture of transparency where feedback is welcomed and encouraged. Netflix also invests heavily in training and development, providing employees opportunities to learn new skills and grow their careers.

Google: Google is renowned for its innovative culture and commitment to continuous learning. The company invests heavily in employee development, offering a wide range of training programs and opportunities for career growth. It also has a culture of open communication, where employees feel comfortable sharing ideas and giving feedback. Google encourages employees to explore new ideas and take risks, and they learn from their failures.

Real-World Applications:

Leadership Coaching: Growth mindset principles can be integrated into leadership coaching programs. By focusing on self-awareness, goal setting, and feedback seeking, coaches can help leaders develop and cultivate a growth mindset within their teams.

Team-Building Exercises: Team-building activities can be designed to promote a growth mindset. For example, a "failure challenge" can encourage teams to embrace challenges, learn from mistakes, and find creative solutions.

Performance Management Systems: Performance management systems can be redesigned to incorporate growth mindset principles. Instead of focusing solely on performance evaluation, they can be used to identify areas for development and create individualized growth plans.

Challenges and Considerations:

Resistance to Change: Shifting from a fixed mindset to a growth mindset requires a significant cultural shift. Some individuals may resist change, mainly if accustomed to a traditional command-and-control leadership style.

Time and Resource Constraints: Cultivating a growth mindset requires significant time and resources. Companies must invest in training programs, development opportunities, and ongoing support to ensure this cultural shift takes root.

Measuring Progress: Measuring the impact of a growth mindset can be challenging. No single metric accurately reflects this mindset, so leaders must rely on a range of qualitative and quantitative data to assess progress.

In a world of constant change and disruption, a growth mindset is no longer a competitive advantage – it's a necessity for survival. By embracing a culture of continuous learning, development, and innovation, leaders can unlock the full potential of their teams and drive their organizations to new heights of success.

Chapter 2

Navigating Remote Work

The Rise of Remote Teams

The rise of remote teams is a testament to the transformative power of technology. It's a phenomenon reshaping how we work, blurring the lines between office life and personal time. This shift has brought a new set of challenges and opportunities for leaders.

Imagine a team scattered across the globe, collaborating on complex projects through virtual meetings, instant messaging, and shared online documents. This once-unimaginable scenario is now commonplace. The internet has revolutionized communication, enabling individuals to connect and work together from anywhere in the world. This newfound flexibility has led to a surge in remote work, with companies of all sizes embracing the benefits.

However, navigating this new landscape requires a different approach to leadership. The traditional command-and-control style, where managers exert direct oversight, doesn't work in a remote setting. Instead, leaders must adapt and embrace new tools and strategies to effectively manage, motivate, and inspire their teams.

One of the most significant changes for leaders is the need to build trust and accountability. When teams are physically separated, it's crucial to establish a foundation of trust. This involves clear communication, setting expectations, and demonstrating your commitment to transparency and honesty. Building trust is a gradual process, but it's essential for fostering a positive and productive remote work environment.

Another challenge lies in fostering a sense of team cohesion and camaraderie when members are geographically dispersed. While virtual coffee breaks and team-building exercises can help, it's vital to cultivate a shared sense of purpose and belonging actively. Leaders can achieve this by promoting open communication channels, celebrating successes together, and fostering a culture of recognition and appreciation.

The shift to remote work also demands a new understanding of communication. Gone are the days of casual hallway conversations and impromptu brainstorming sessions.

Leaders must master the art of virtual communication, utilizing various tools and techniques to ensure clear and compelling messaging. This includes leveraging video conferencing, asynchronous communication platforms, and project management software.

However, it's not just about technology; it's about understanding the nuances of virtual communication. Leaders need to be mindful of time zones, cultural differences, and potential misinterpretations. They must learn to be more explicit in their communication, providing context and clarity to avoid confusion.

Navigating remote work challenges also involves addressing the potential for isolation and burnout. While remote work offers flexibility and a better work-life balance for many, it's essential to acknowledge the potential downsides. Leaders must proactively create opportunities for social interaction, encourage breaks, and promote healthy work-life integration.

The rise of remote teams presents a unique opportunity for leadership to evolve. It's a chance to rethink traditional approaches and embrace a more collaborative, inclusive, and technology-driven style. This shift requires adaptability, empathy, and a deep understanding of the challenges and opportunities presented by remote work. By embracing these principles, leaders can build strong, resilient, highly productive remote teams.

Let's delve into a few concrete examples that illustrate the complexities and rewards of leading in the remote work era:

Example 1: The Rise of Remote-First Companies

Companies like GitLab and Zapier have embraced a remote-first approach, hiring talent globally and building their entire operations around remote work. This model has allowed them to tap into a diverse pool of talent, reduce geographical limitations, and promote inclusivity.

However, it also demands strong communication strategies, clear expectations, and robust onboarding processes to ensure seamless integration of new employees.

Example 2: The Importance of Communication in Remote Teams

Imagine a project team working on a complex software development project across multiple time zones.

Without effective communication, confusion, delays, and misunderstandings are inevitable. Leaders in this context must prioritize regular communication, utilize project management tools, and facilitate frequent virtual meetings to ensure everyone is on the same page.

Example 3: Fostering Remote Team Culture

A company headquartered in New York has a team of engineers working remotely from India. To foster a sense of belonging and community, the company organizes virtual team events, encourages social interactions in online channels, and celebrates achievements together. This proactive approach helps to combat feelings of isolation and create a more cohesive remote work environment.

Example 4: Overcoming Remote Work Challenges

A marketing team struggles to maintain momentum and motivation in a remote setting. The leader recognizes the potential for burnout and implements strategies to address this. These include encouraging regular breaks, promoting a healthy work-life balance, and offering professional development and growth opportunities.

Example 5: Leading Through Empathy in Remote Teams

A team leader observes that one of their remote employees seems withdrawn and disengaged. They contact the employee, inquiring about their well-being and offering support. By demonstrating empathy and understanding, the leader helps to address potential issues before they escalate.

These examples highlight the key elements of effective remote leadership: building trust, fostering collaboration, mastering virtual communication, addressing challenges, and prioritizing employee well-being. By embracing these principles, leaders can create thriving remote teams that are innovative, productive and engaged.

As we move forward in a world increasingly dominated by remote work, the ability to lead effectively in a virtual environment will become more crucial than ever. This chapter has provided a framework for navigating this new terrain, equipping leaders with the tools and strategies to thrive in the era of remote teams.

Tools for Effective Communication

In the digital age, remote work has become the norm for many organizations, presenting both opportunities and challenges for leaders. Effective communication is the lifeblood of any successful team, but it takes on even greater importance in the context of remote work. The distance between team members can create communication barriers and lead to misunderstandings if not addressed thoughtfully. This is where technology steps in, offering a wealth of tools designed to bridge the gap and facilitate seamless collaboration.

Imagine a team scattered across the globe, collaborating on a complex project. They must brainstorm ideas, share files, conduct meetings, and stay aligned on goals. This is where the right technology tools become indispensable, transforming virtual interactions into a productive and engaging experience.

Video Conferencing: The Face-to-Face Experience, Virtually

Video conferencing platforms like Zoom, Microsoft Teams, and Google Meet have revolutionized how we communicate remotely. They bring the human element to virtual interactions, allowing team members to see each other's faces, read their nonverbal cues, and create a more personal connection. This visual aspect is critical for building trust and fostering a sense of camaraderie.

Beyond the basic video call, these platforms offer a range of features that enhance collaboration. Screen sharing enables teams to present ideas, share documents, and collaborate on projects in real time. Interactive whiteboards allow teams to brainstorm, annotate documents, and work together on a shared canvas, mirroring the experience of a physical whiteboard in a traditional office setting.

Instant Messaging: Keeping the Conversation Flowing

Instant messaging (IM) tools like Slack, Microsoft Teams, and Google Chat have become the go-to communication channels for quick, informal interactions. They allow teams to communicate instantly, share updates, ask quick questions, and keep the conversation flowing seamlessly. IM platforms also provide channels for specific projects, teams, or departments, enabling focused communication and reducing email clutter.

These tools often integrate with other applications, allowing teams to access and share information from different sources within the same platform. For example, integrating Slack with

Google Drive allows seamless file sharing and direct collaboration within the IM channel. This integration streamlines workflows and eliminates the need to switch between different platforms.

Project Management Tools: Staying Organized and On Track

Project management tools like Asana, Trello, and Monday.com are essential for keeping remote teams organized and on track. They provide a central hub for managing tasks, deadlines, progress, and communication. Team members can assign tasks, track progress, collaborate on projects, and receive deadline notifications.

These tools also facilitate transparency and accountability, ensuring everyone knows project goals, milestones, and progress. Visual dashboards provide a clear overview of project status, helping leaders identify potential bottlenecks or areas that require additional attention.

Collaboration Platforms: A Unified Work Environment

Collaboration platforms like Google Workspace and Microsoft 365 offer a suite of tools designed to enhance remote team productivity. They include features like shared document editing, cloud storage, email communication, and video conferencing, all within a unified platform. This integration eliminates the need for multiple accounts and facilitates a seamless workflow.

Imagine a team working on a presentation. They can collaborate on the document simultaneously in real-time, using Google Docs or Microsoft Word. They can then access and share the finished presentation through Google Drive or OneDrive, ensuring all team members can access the latest version. Finally, they can schedule a video conference using Google Meet or Microsoft Teams to review the presentation and make final adjustments. This streamlined process eliminates the need for multiple platforms and ensures efficient collaboration.

Communication Best Practices

While technology provides powerful tools for remote communication, it's essential to implement best practices to ensure effective and productive interactions. Here are some key considerations:

Overcommunicate: In a remote setting, effective communication is crucial to avoid misunderstandings. Provide clear and concise instructions, confirm understanding, and reiterate important points. Regular check-ins and updates help keep everyone aligned and informed.

Be mindful of time zones: Different time zones can pose challenges in scheduling meetings and coordinating efforts.

Be mindful of your team members' time zones and schedule meetings at times that are convenient for everyone. Consider using online scheduling tools that automatically take time zone differences into account.

Embrace asynchronous communication: Only some things need to be a live conversation. Encourage asynchronous communication for less urgent matters, allowing team members to respond conveniently. This flexibility can benefit remote teams with members in different time zones.

Foster a culture of transparency: Transparency is crucial for building trust and fostering a positive team dynamic.

Encourage open communication, share updates regularly, and be transparent about project progress and challenges.

Invest in communication training: Consider providing communication training to your team, especially for those new to remote work. This training can cover topics like virtual communication etiquette, active listening, and conflict resolution.

The Evolution of Communication

Technology continues to evolve rapidly, offering new and innovative tools for remote collaboration. Artificial Intelligence (AI) is already playing a significant role in enhancing communication efficiency. AI-powered chatbots can automate routine tasks, answer frequently asked questions, and provide instant support to team members. AI can also analyze communication patterns and identify potential areas for improvement, helping leaders optimize team communication.

The future of remote work communication will likely be even more sophisticated, with personalized communication experiences, real-time translation, and seamless integration across different platforms. Leaders must stay abreast of these technological advancements and adapt their communication strategies accordingly.

Conclusion

The right technology tools and communication best practices can transform remote work from a logistical challenge into a productive and engaging experience. By embracing these technologies and fostering a culture of open communication, leaders can create a strong team dynamic and achieve remarkable results, regardless of physical distance.

Remember, successful communication is the cornerstone of any successful remote team.

Building Trust and Accountability

Trust is the foundation of successful collaboration in remote work. It's the invisible thread that binds virtual teams together, fostering a sense of shared purpose and accountability even when colleagues are miles apart. Without trust, remote work can devolve into a tangled web of suspicion, micromanagement, and diminished productivity. Building trust in a virtual environment requires a conscious effort, a shift in mindset, and adopting specific strategies that acknowledge the unique challenges of remote collaboration.

One of the foundational pillars of trust in any team, remote or otherwise, is open and transparent communication. In a virtual setting, this becomes even more crucial. When communication channels are clear and consistent, it allows team members to stay informed about projects, deadlines, and each other's progress. The absence of face-to-face interaction necessitates a heightened awareness of communication styles and the potential for misinterpretation. Tools like video conferencing, instant messaging, and project management platforms can bridge the physical distance, but it's essential to establish clear communication protocols and expectations. This means defining response times, preferred communication channels for different inquiries, and fostering a culture of open dialogue where questions and concerns are encouraged, not stifled.

Beyond communication, trust flourishes when there is a shared understanding of roles and responsibilities within the team. Clearly defined expectations, both individual and team-wide, serve as a roadmap for success. When everyone knows their

contribution to the overall project and how their work inter-
connects with others, it fosters a sense of shared ownership
and responsibility. This transparency reduces ambiguity and
minimizes the potential for misunderstandings or duplicated
efforts. Setting clear goals and breaking down large projects
into manageable tasks, coupled with regular check-ins and
progress updates, contributes to a culture of accountability.

Building trust in a remote setting also involves actively cultivating a sense of community and belonging. It's about creating a
virtual space where team members feel connected, valued, and
engaged. This might involve regular virtual team-building activities, informal social gatherings, or even dedicated online fo-
rums for non-work-related discussions. These seemingly
insignificant initiatives play a vital role in fostering a sense of
camaraderie and mutual support, which in turn strengthens the
bonds of trust within the team.

Without physical proximity, trust often relies heavily on individual character and reliability. Leaders play a pivotal role in
cultivating this trust by setting an example.

When leaders demonstrate integrity, honesty, and consistency
in their actions, they create an environment where team members feel comfortable trusting each other.

Trust involves being transparent about decisions, acknowledging mistakes, and actively seeking feedback. Leaders can create
a culture of mutual respect and trust by actively listening to
team members, recognizing their contributions, and providing
constructive feedback.

However, building trust is a continuous journey, not a destination. It requires ongoing effort, vigilance, and adaptability.

There will be instances where misunderstandings arise, deadlines are missed, or unexpected challenges emerge. These are opportunities to strengthen the bonds of trust, not to weaken them. By approaching these situations with open communication, empathy, and a willingness to learn from mistakes, teams can overcome challenges and emerge with a more profound sense of trust and resilience.

In remote work, trust is not merely a desirable trait; it's a fundamental requirement for success. It's the invisible glue that holds virtual teams together, enabling them to navigate the challenges of distance and achieve remarkable things. By actively cultivating trust through open communication, clear expectations, a sense of community, and leadership that sets the right example, organizations can unlock the full potential of their remote workforce.

Beyond building trust, accountability plays an equally critical role in the success of remote teams. It's the fuel that drives performance, ensuring that commitments are met, goals are achieved, and everyone is working towards a shared vision. Without direct supervision, accountability often relies on self-motivation, a sense of shared purpose, and transparent performance metrics.

Leaders play a crucial role in fostering accountability by setting clear performance expectations and providing regular feedback. This doesn't have to be a rigid process; it can be a collaborative dialogue where leaders and team members discuss progress, identify areas for improvement, and agree on the next steps. Transparency in performance metrics and clear communication around goals and objectives are essential for establishing a culture of accountability.

Furthermore, using technology can be a valuable tool for enhancing accountability in remote teams. Project management software, time-tracking tools, and collaborative workspaces can provide valuable insights into individual and team progress. By leveraging these tools, leaders can clearly understand individual contributions, identify potential bottlenecks, and provide timely support. However, it's important to remember that technology is a means to an end, not an end in itself. The focus should always remain on achieving the desired outcomes, not simply tracking progress.

Accountability also thrives on a culture of shared ownership and responsibility. When team members feel a sense of ownership over their work and the overall project, they are more likely to take accountability for their actions and strive for excellence. This can be fostered by empowering team members to make decisions, take initiative, and own their areas of responsibility.

Additionally, regular team check-ins, both formal and informal, provide opportunities for team members to update each other on their progress, discuss challenges, and collaborate on solutions. These interactions, even if they're brief, can reinforce accountability and ensure that everyone is aligned on goals and priorities.

While technology and transparent processes are essential, accountability is ultimately driven by individual commitment and a sense of collective purpose. Leaders play a crucial role in nurturing this sense of purpose by clearly communicating the team's vision, values, and impact. When team members understand the significance of their work and its contribution to the organization's broader goals, they are more likely to feel a sense of ownership and responsibility for their actions.

Trust and accountability create a robust foundation for success in remote teams. Trust fosters a sense of psychological safety, allowing team members to feel comfortable taking risks, sharing ideas, and supporting each other. Accountability provides the framework for ensuring those ideas are translated into action, and everyone works towards a shared goal.

Together, trust and accountability enable remote teams to thrive, even without physical proximity. By actively cultivating these qualities, organizations can unlock the full potential of their remote workforce and create a culture of collaboration, innovation, and high performance.

Overcoming Remote Work Challenges

The transition to remote work has brought about new challenges for leaders. While remote work offers numerous benefits, it also presents unique obstacles that require innovative solutions. Let's dive into these challenges and explore practical strategies to overcome them:

Communication Gaps: Imagine this: You're leading a virtual team meeting, and you're bombarded with messages in the chat. You're trying to explain a complex project to your team, but there's a lag in the video call, and some team members are not responding. Feeling frustrated and misunderstood is easy when you can't see people's reactions in real-time. This is just one example of the communication challenges that remote teams face.

Solution: Embrace a multi-modal approach to communication. Don't rely solely on video conferencing. Use a combination of tools like instant messaging, project management software, and even old-fashioned email to ensure that everyone stays informed. Regular check-ins, even just a quick 15-minute chat, can help build stronger connections and keep everyone on the same page.

Lack of Face-to-Face Interaction: Many leaders miss the spontaneous interactions that happen in traditional offices. The casual hallway chats, impromptu brainstorming sessions, and team lunches all contribute to a sense of camaraderie and team spirit. Remote work can feel isolating, especially for new hires who have yet to have the chance to build relationships in person.

Solution: Make time for virtual team-building activities. Plan online games, virtual happy hours, or even group book clubs. Encourage team members to share their personal lives and interests to foster a sense of connection. These activities can help bridge the physical gap and build a stronger team culture.

Maintaining Motivation and Engagement: Keeping remote teams motivated and engaged is challenging when they're not physically present in the office. Distractions at home, feelings of isolation, and a lack of social interaction can all lead to decreased productivity and engagement.

Solution: Recognize and celebrate achievements, no matter how small. Provide regular feedback and acknowledge individual contributions. Set clear expectations and goals, and empower team members to take ownership of their work. Consider offering flexible work schedules to accommodate different lifestyles and personal needs.

Building Trust and Accountability: Trust and accountability are essential for any team but are particularly crucial in remote work environments. When you can't physically see your team members, gauging their progress and commitment is more difficult.

Solution: Implement clear performance metrics and track progress regularly. Encourage open and honest communication. Provide team members with the tools and resources they need to succeed. Celebrate successes and address challenges openly and constructively.

Managing Time Zones and Schedules: Working with remote teams across different time zones can be a logistical nightmare. Scheduling meetings that work for everyone, responding to emails at odd hours, and coordinating deadlines can feel like a constant balancing act.

Solution: Use scheduling tools that account for time zones. Communicate clearly about your availability and expected response times. Be flexible and understanding of different schedules. Consider using asynchronous communication tools for tasks that don't require real-time interaction.

Burnout and Work-Life Balance: Remote work can blur the lines between work and personal life. It's easy to feel overwhelmed when you're always accessible and expected to be available at all hours. This can lead to burnout and decreased well-being.

Solution: Encourage your team to take regular breaks. Set clear boundaries between work and personal time. Promote a culture of well-being and encourage team members to prioritize their mental and physical health.

The Role of Technology: Technology is both a blessing and a curse in remote work. It allows for seamless communication and collaboration but can also be a source of distraction and burnout.

Solution: Choose the right tools for the job. Not all technology is created equal. Invest in tools that enhance productivity, communication, and collaboration, and ensure your team is comfortable using them.

Leadership in a Remote Environment: The leadership style that worked in a traditional office setting may not be effective in a remote environment.

Leaders must adapt their approach to manage and motivate remote teams effectively.

Solution: Focus on clear communication, empathy, and trust. Provide regular feedback and recognition. Encourage open and honest communication. Create a sense of community and belonging, even from a distance.

Building a Strong Remote Team Culture: Remote teams must work together to create a strong team culture. This requires conscious effort and proactive leadership.

Solution: Organize virtual team-building activities. Encourage social interaction among team members.

Celebrate successes and share milestones. Promote a culture of inclusivity and respect for diverse perspectives.

Overcoming Remote Work Challenges with Technology:

Technology plays a crucial role in overcoming the challenges of remote work. Various technologies, from communication tools to project management software, can help teams collaborate effectively and maintain productivity.

Collaboration Platforms: Platforms like Microsoft Teams, Slack, and Google Workspace enable real-time communication, file sharing, and project management. These tools facilitate seamless collaboration and keep everyone on the same page.

Video Conferencing Tools: Tools like Zoom, Google Meet, and Microsoft Teams allow for video conferencing, screen sharing, and virtual meetings. These tools enhance team communication and foster a sense of connection.

Project Management Software: Tools like Asana, Trello, and Jira help teams manage projects, track progress, and assign tasks. They provide a centralized platform for organizing work and ensuring accountability.

Time Management Tools: Tools like Todoist, Asana, and Google Calendar help team members manage their time effectively, prioritize tasks, and avoid distractions. These tools promote productivity and streamline workflow.

Communication and Collaboration Tools: Tools like Slack, Microsoft Teams, and Zoom are essential for communication and collaboration in remote teams. They enable instant messaging, video conferencing, and file sharing, facilitating seamless communication and helping teams stay connected.

The Importance of Human Connection:

Despite technological advancements, human connection remains essential for remote team success. Building trust, fostering a sense of belonging, and celebrating achievements are crucial to creating a positive and productive remote work environment.

Virtual Team-Building Activities: Virtual team-building activities can help remote teams bond and build relationships. Online games, virtual happy hours, or even group book clubs can foster a sense of camaraderie and connection.

Regular Check-Ins and Feedback: Leaders should prioritize regular check-ins with team members to ensure they feel supported and engaged. Regular feedback and recognition for individual contributions can boost morale and motivation.

Creating a Culture of Open Communication: Open and honest communication is vital for remote teams. Encourage team members to share their challenges, ideas, and feedback openly and constructively. This helps build trust and transparency within the team.

Celebrating Successes and Milestones: Celebrating successes and milestones, no matter how small, can boost team morale and create a sense of achievement. It's essential to acknowledge and appreciate each team member's contributions.

A Balanced Approach to Remote Work:

Finding a balance between technology and human connection is crucial for successful remote work. While technology can facilitate collaboration and communication, it's equally important to prioritize the human element of teamwork. Leaders should create a culture that values technological efficiency and genuine human interaction.

Overcoming the challenges of remote work requires a combination of practical strategies, technological solutions, and a focus on building strong team dynamics. By embracing communication, fostering trust, and prioritizing well-being, leaders can create a thriving remote work environment where teams can collaborate effectively, achieve goals, and contribute to the organization's success.

Fostering Remote Team Culture

Building a vibrant and engaging team culture when everyone is geographically dispersed can be tricky. It's like trying to build a campfire in a virtual world – you need the proper kindling and a steady hand to keep the flames burning bright. But fear not; it's not impossible, and there are plenty of ways to cultivate a strong team spirit despite the physical distance.

Imagine you're building a virtual office, a space where people can come together, share ideas, and feel connected, even if they're miles apart. The first step is to **create a shared sense of purpose and identity**. This is the foundation of any strong team culture, whether in person or online. Think about it like a virtual clubhouse – everyone knows the rules, the values, and what it means to be a part of the team.

Communication is key. We're not just talking about email chains and endless chat messages; we're talking **about real conversations, genuine connections, and shared moments.** Think about the tools you can use to replicate spontaneous conversations and water-cooler chats in a physical office. Video conferencing is a must-have, allowing faces and voices to bridge the distance. Regular team meetings, whether daily stand-up meetings or weekly brainstorming sessions are essential.

Remember, **building trust is paramount in remote teams**. It's like building a bridge over a digital chasm. Transparency is key. Open communication, clear expectations, and regular feedback foster trust and accountability; make sure everyone has the opportunity to voice their opinions and contribute their ideas, regardless of their location.

To **cultivate a sense of belonging,** you must create opportunities for team members to connect personally. This can be through virtual social gatherings, online games, or shared projects encouraging collaboration and interaction. Consider incorporating team-building activities promoting social connection, like online quizzes, virtual scavenger hunts, or even collaborative cooking demonstrations.

Celebrate successes together, even if it's just a virtual high-five. Recognize and acknowledge individual contributions and celebrate milestones, no matter how small.

These moments of recognition can go a long way in fostering a sense of shared accomplishment and team spirit.

Remember, **culture isn't just something you build; it's something you nurture**. It's about creating a space where everyone feels valued, respected, and connected, even working from different locations. So, go forth and cultivate your virtual team culture, and remember, a little creativity and genuine connection can go a long way!

Now, let's examine some real-world examples of companies that have successfully fostered a remote team culture.

Buffer is a prime example. This social media scheduling platform has a fully remote team, and they prioritize communication, transparency, and a strong sense of community. They have regular online team meetings, utilize tools like Slack for seamless communication, and even host virtual team retreats to foster connection. They also emphasize open communication and encourage employees to share feedback and suggestions.

GitHub, the popular code hosting platform, is another excellent example. They've embraced remote work and built a thriving culture that values flexibility, collaboration, and diversity.

They use asynchronous communication tools, encourage regular check-ins, and invest in professional development opportunities for their remote employees. GitHub also prioritizes building trust through transparency, clear communication, and shared goals.

These examples highlight that building a remote team culture is not a myth but a reality. With a little effort and dedication, any team can thrive in a virtual environment, fostering a sense of connection, collaboration, and camaraderie.

Here are some additional tips for fostering remote team culture:

Set clear expectations and guidelines: Ensure everyone is on the same page regarding communication protocols, deadlines, and work responsibilities.

Embrace asynchronous communication: Use tools that allow team members to work at their own pace, responding to messages and completing tasks when it is convenient for them.

Create a shared virtual workspace: Use tools like Trello, Asana, or Monday.com to manage projects, track progress, and keep everyone informed.

Invest in team-building activities: To promote team bonding, organize virtual happy hours, online games, or even virtual escape room experiences.

Recognize and reward individual contributions: Celebrate successes and acknowledge individual achievements to foster a sense of accomplishment.

Encourage mentorship and peer support: Connect team members through mentoring programs or peer support groups to provide guidance and encouragement.

Promote diversity and inclusion: Create a welcoming environment where everyone feels valued and respected, regardless of background or location.

By embracing these strategies and fostering a communication, collaboration, and connection culture, you can create a thriving remote team culture that drives success and strengthens your organization.

Chapter 3

Building Resilient Teams

Understanding Team Resilience

Imagine a team navigating a turbulent sea. They face unexpected storms, strong currents, and shifting tides. Yet, they weather the challenges, adapting their course and working together to reach their destination. This is the essence of team resilience – the ability to bounce back from adversity, learn from setbacks, and emerge stronger.

Teams encounter constant change and disruption in the fast-paced business world, particularly in the digital age. They face technological advancements, shifting market dynamics, and evolving customer needs. Teams that can weather these storms and emerge stronger are the ones that truly thrive.

Resilience is not merely the absence of setbacks. It's about how a team responds to those setbacks—the ability to adapt, learn, and grow. It's the collective strength that allows a team to overcome obstacles, maintain focus on its goals, and continue to perform at its best.

Think of a product development team facing a major deadline. They encounter a critical bug in their software just days before launch. A less resilient team might panic, leading to rushed fixes and potential compromises in quality.

A resilient team, however, embraces the challenge. They work together to identify the root cause of the bug, implement a solution, and adjust their schedule to ensure a successful launch.

Resilience is about more than technical skills or problem-solving abilities. It's also about the team's emotional intelligence, communication skills, and ability to collaborate effectively. Resilient teams have a strong sense of trust and shared purpose, allowing them to navigate difficulties with open communication and a collective mindset.

Here's how resilience plays a crucial role in team dynamics and performance:

Enhanced Performance: Resilient teams are better equipped to handle unexpected challenges, reducing the impact of disruptions on their productivity and performance.

They can maintain their focus and momentum even when faced with setbacks.

Increased Innovation: When teams feel secure and supported, they are more likely to take risks and experiment with new ideas. Resilience allows them to embrace failure as a learning opportunity, fostering a culture of experimentation and innovation.

Improved Communication: Resilience requires open communication and clear feedback. Resilient teams are better at sharing information, acknowledging challenges, and working collaboratively to find solutions.

Stronger Relationships: Resilient teams build stronger relationships based on trust, mutual respect, and a shared understanding of each other's strengths and weaknesses.

They know they can rely on each other, even during challenging times.

The ability to bounce back from setbacks is not an inherent trait of any team. It's a skill that needs to be nurtured and developed. Just as individual resilience is built through self-awareness, emotional regulation, and optimism, team resilience requires a conscious effort from leaders and team members.

Think of it as a journey of continuous learning and growth.

Teams need to identify their vulnerabilities, develop strategies to mitigate them, and constantly strive to enhance their ability to navigate challenges and thrive in adversity.

In the next section, we'll explore practical strategies for building team resilience, focusing on how leaders can play a vital role in fostering this crucial attribute. We'll also delve into real-world examples of teams that have demonstrated resilience, showcasing the impact of this critical factor in achieving business success.

Strategies for Resilience Building

In the context of teams, resilience isn't just about bouncing back from challenges; it's about the ability to adapt, learn, and thrive in the face of uncertainty and adversity. It's about recognizing that change is constant, embracing it, and even turning it into an advantage. Imagine a team that navigates through a sudden market shift, a global pandemic, or a technological disruption—not only does it survive, it emerges more decisive, innovative, and even more tightly knit than before. That's the power of resilience.

Building resilient teams isn't a magic trick; it requires a conscious effort and a shift in mindset. Think of it as building muscle—you must exercise it consistently and push it to its limits to see real growth. Here are some practical strategies that you, as a leader, can implement to foster resilience in your team:

1. Cultivate a Culture of Open Communication:

Transparency is the bedrock of a resilient team. Imagine a team member who struggles with a task but is afraid to speak up. This can lead to frustration, missed deadlines, and resentment. Open communication breaks down these barriers. Encourage team members to share their concerns, challenges, and even their successes. Create a space where honest feedback is valued and where everyone feels comfortable expressing their opinions without fear of judgment.

2. Embrace failure as a Learning Opportunity:

Failure is not the enemy; it's a valuable teacher. In a world of constant change, some projects will inevitably falter, some strategies will fail, and some experiments won't yield the desired results. The key is to approach these failures with a growth mindset. Instead of focusing on blame, encourage your team to analyze the situation, identify the root causes of the failure, and learn from the experience. This process of reflection and adaptation strengthens the team's resilience, allowing them to apply those lessons to future endeavors.

3. Foster Diversity of Thought and Backgrounds:

A diverse team in terms of perspectives, skills, and backgrounds is better equipped to handle challenges.

Different perspectives allow for a broader range of solutions to be considered, and diverse experiences can provide valuable insights during times of uncertainty. For example, a team of individuals with expertise in different industries or markets might be better positioned to adapt to rapid industry shifts than a team with a more homogeneous background.

4. Encourage Continuous Learning and Development:

The world of technology is ever-evolving, and so are the skills needed to thrive in it. As a leader, you must create an environment that prioritizes continuous learning. This could involve providing access to online courses, sponsoring conferences, encouraging participation in workshops, or even setting aside time for team members to explore new tools and technologies. By staying ahead of the curve, your team will be better equipped to navigate the complexities of the digital landscape.

5. Build Strong Relationships and Trust:

Trust is the glue that holds a resilient team together. When team members trust each other, they are more likely to communicate openly and honestly, support each other through tough times, and collaborate effectively. Build trust by consistently demonstrating integrity, fairness, and respect for your team members. Foster a sense of community and belonging, encouraging team members to connect with each other both professionally and personally.

6. Empower Team Members to Take Ownership:

Micromanaging can stifle creativity and innovation, making it harder for a team to adapt to change. Empower your team members to take ownership of their work and make decisions aligning with the team's goals. Provide them with the resources and support they need to succeed, but trust their judgment and allow them to take risks. This fosters a sense of responsibility and helps identify and cultivate future leaders within the team.

7. Implement Regular Team Retrospectives:

Regular team retrospectives are essential for assessing the team's performance, identifying areas for improvement, and celebrating successes. These sessions provide an opportunity to reflect on the team's strengths and weaknesses, identify patterns in their approach to challenges, and discuss how they can work together more effectively. It's important to focus on constructive feedback and solutions, avoid blame, and foster a culture of continuous improvement.

8. Seek External Feedback and Mentorship:

Don't be afraid to look outside your team for fresh perspectives. Seek feedback from external stakeholders, mentors, or industry experts. This can provide valuable insights that might not be readily apparent within the team. A mentor can offer guidance, support, and a sounding board for your team's challenges, helping them to refine their approach and develop strategies for overcoming obstacles.

9. Embrace Technology and Innovation:

In the digital age, staying ahead of the technological curve is not just an advantage—it's essential for survival. Encourage your team to experiment with new tools and technologies, embrace automation, and explore ways to leverage technology to streamline processes and improve efficiency. This could involve adopting project management software, using collaborative tools for communication, or even exploring artificial intelligence applications.

10. Practice Mindfulness and Stress Management:

Resilience isn't just about the team as a whole; it's also about the well-being of individual team members. Encourage your team to practice mindfulness and stress management techniques like meditation, yoga, or deep breathing exercises. These practices can help reduce stress, enhance focus, and improve overall mental well-being, making them more resilient to workplace challenges.

Real-World Examples:

Example 1: Spotify's Agile Approach

Spotify, the music streaming giant, has built a reputation for its agile and adaptable approach to product development.

They have implemented a highly decentralized structure, empowering teams to take ownership of their projects and make quick decisions. This flexibility has allowed Spotify to respond rapidly to changing market conditions and to innovate at a breakneck pace.

Example 2: Airbnb's Crisis Management

In the early days of the COVID-19 pandemic, Airbnb faced a significant crisis as travel reached a standstill. The company responded by quickly implementing several initiatives to support its hosts and guests, including a flexible cancellation policy and a program to help hosts diversify their income streams. This swift and decisive action helped to preserve the platform's core value proposition and ultimately contributed to its recovery.

Example 3: Google's Emphasis on Employee Well-being

Google is known for its focus on employee well-being. It offers generous benefits, flexible work arrangements, and a variety of programs aimed at reducing stress and fostering a positive work environment. This commitment to employee well-being has resulted in a highly engaged and productive workforce, making Google a formidable competitor in the tech industry.

Building a Resilient Team is an Ongoing Journey

Building a resilient team is not a one-time event; it's an ongoing journey that requires continuous effort and adaptation. By fostering a culture of open communication, embracing failure as a learning opportunity, and empowering your team members to take ownership of their work, you can create a team that is adaptable to change and thrives in the face of adversity. In today's rapidly changing world, resilience isn't just a desirable trait—it's a necessity for success. The teams that embrace resilience will be the ones who shape the future, leaving a lasting impact on their industry and beyond.

The Role of Leadership in Resilience

In the dynamic world of modern leadership, resilience isn't just a nice-to-have quality; it's a necessity. Resilient teams can weather storms, adapt to change, and emerge stronger than ever. But what does it take to build such a team? The answer lies, in part, with the leaders themselves. They are the architects of resilience, the guiding force that sets the foundation for a team that can handle anything.

Imagine a team facing a significant setback. A crucial project has been delayed, a key client has pulled out, or a competitor has launched a disruptive innovation. In this moment, the leader's role is critical. They can't simply offer platitudes or dismiss the challenge. Instead, they must embody calm amidst the storm, the steady hand guiding the team back to solid ground.

Here's how leaders can empower their teams to become resilient:

Embrace Vulnerability: Leaders who are open about their struggles and challenges create a safe space for their team members to do the same. This authenticity fosters trust and encourages open communication, which are critical ingredients for resilience.

Lead by Example: The best way to instill resilience in a team is to demonstrate it yourself. When faced with setbacks, leaders should show their team how to bounce back, learn from mistakes, and move forward with determination. Their actions speak louder than their words.

Foster a Growth Mindset: Resilience isn't about avoiding failure but learning and growing from it. Leaders should cultivate a culture where mistakes are seen as opportunities for improvement, not as defeats. This mindset encourages experimentation, risk-taking, and continuous learning, all essential for team resilience.

Encourage Collaboration and Support: Resilient teams are built on strong relationships and mutual support. Leaders should actively encourage team members to share their strengths, collaborate on solutions, and offer each other encouragement. This shared sense of purpose and belonging is a powerful antidote to adversity.

Provide Clear Direction and Support: In times of uncertainty, teams need clarity and guidance. Leaders should articulate a clear vision for the future, setting goals and milestones that provide direction and focus. They should also provide the resources and support necessary for the team to navigate challenges.

Recognize and Celebrate Successes: Resilience isn't just about surviving difficult times; it's also about celebrating achievements and recognizing the team's hard work.

Leaders should acknowledge and appreciate the efforts of their team members, particularly during challenging periods.

This reinforces the importance of perseverance and strengthens team morale.

Invest in Continuous Learning and Development: The modern business landscape is constantly evolving, so leaders need to invest in their team members' continuous learning and development. This could include providing opportunities for skill-building, attending workshops, or taking on new challenges. By keeping their skills sharp, team members are better equipped to adapt to change and overcome obstacles.

Build a Culture of Open Communication: Resilient teams are characterized by open and honest communication.

Leaders should create an environment where team members feel comfortable sharing concerns, ideas, and feedback.

Regular team meetings, one-on-one check-ins, and open channels of communication foster transparency and build trust.

Promote Psychological Safety: A key aspect of resilience is psychological safety, a sense of security, and trust within a team. Leaders should create an environment where team members feel comfortable taking risks, voicing dissenting opinions, and making mistakes without fear of judgment or reprisal. This psychological safety allows creativity, innovation, and the freedom to learn from mistakes.

Building resilient teams is an ongoing process, not a one-time event. Leaders must actively foster this attribute, constantly nurturing a culture that embraces change, encourages growth, and celebrates success. By embodying resilience and actively promoting it within their teams, leaders can create a powerhouse of talent capable of overcoming challenges and achieving extraordinary results.

Let's look at a few real-world examples of how leaders have successfully fostered team resilience:

Jeff Bezos at Amazon: Bezos is known for his relentless focus on innovation and customer-centricity. He instilled a culture of experimentation and continuous improvement at Amazon, encouraging his team to embrace failure as a learning opportunity. This "fail fast, learn faster" approach has helped Amazon navigate the ever-changing world of e-commerce and remain a global leader.

Satya Nadella at Microsoft: When Nadella took the helm at Microsoft, he shifted the company's culture from a rigid, hierarchical structure to one that emphasized collaboration, empathy, and a growth mindset. He empowered his team to take risks, experiment with new technologies, and embrace the changing digital landscape. This cultural shift helped Microsoft regain its footing in the tech industry and become a leading cloud computing provider.

Sheryl Sandberg at Facebook: Sandberg is known for her focus on building strong, diverse teams. At Facebook, she prioritized initiatives like women in leadership and promoting a culture of inclusivity. This focus on diversity and inclusion created a more resilient team, able to draw on a broader range of perspectives and experiences to navigate challenges.

The leaders mentioned above demonstrate that resilience isn't just about surviving tough times; it's about thriving in them. By fostering a culture of collaboration, learning, and growth, leaders can empower their teams to not only withstand adversity but also to emerge from it stronger and more capable than ever before.

Case Studies in Team Resilience

Unexpected twists and turns often mark the journey of a resilient team. It's about navigating storms, bouncing back from setbacks, and emerging stronger than before. But what exactly does it mean for a team to be resilient, and how can leaders foster that resilience?

Let's dive into some real-world examples that showcase the power of resilient teams in action.

The Story of SpaceX's Falcon 9 Rocket:

2016, the world watched in awe as SpaceX's Falcon 9 rocket exploded during a launch test. It was a catastrophic failure that could have quickly incapacitated the company, but instead, it became a defining moment in their journey. The team, led by the visionary Elon Musk, stayed calm under pressure. They meticulously analyzed the cause of the explosion, identified the design flaw, and re-engineered the rocket. This relentless dedication to problem-solving, fueled by a commitment to their mission, allowed SpaceX to recover, innovate, and push the boundaries of space exploration further.

The Triumph of the Boston Red Sox:

The Boston Red Sox team was known for their curse, a long streak of failed attempts to win the World Series. For 86 years, the curse haunted them. However, in 2004, a resilient Red Sox team defied the odds. They faced a seemingly insurmountable 3-0 deficit in the American League Championship Series, a situation many considered impossible to overcome. Yet, fueled by a belief in their abilities and a determined spirit, they fought back, winning the next four games to reach the World Series. This extraordinary comeback showcased the power of unwavering belief, teamwork, and resilience in the face of adversity.

The Resilience of the Chilean Miners:

In 2010, a catastrophic mine collapse trapped 33 miners deep beneath the Chilean desert. The world watched with bated breath as a rescue operation, dubbed "Plan A," was launched to bring them home. The miners, faced with the daunting reality of their situation, displayed remarkable resilience.

They formed a tight-knit community, sharing meager resources, supporting each other's emotional well-being, and even organizing themselves to manage their time and activities. The strength of their bond, their commitment to survival, and their unwavering hope kept them going until they were finally rescued after 69 days.

Lessons from Resilience:

These are just a few examples of teams that demonstrated exceptional resilience in facing challenges. What can we learn from their stories?

- Resilience is not just about overcoming setbacks; it's about adapting and growing through them.

- Strong leadership is crucial in fostering resilience. Leaders who create a culture of trust, open communication, and shared responsibility empower their teams to face challenges head-on.

- Resilience is a continuous process, not a one-time event.

- It requires ongoing effort to build strong relationships, develop problem-solving skills, and adapt to changing circumstances.

Beyond the Case Studies:

The examples we've explored illustrate the tangible impact of resilient teams. But how can leaders cultivate resilience in their teams? It's about more than just inspiring speeches and pep talks. It requires a strategic approach that incorporates various elements:

Building Trust and Psychological Safety: A resilient team starts with a foundation of trust and psychological safety.

This means creating an environment where team members feel comfortable sharing their ideas, admitting mistakes, and seeking support without fear of judgment.

Fostering a Growth Mindset: Encouraging a growth mindset is crucial for resilience. It means promoting a culture of continuous learning, where setbacks are viewed as opportunities for growth and development.

Promoting Communication and Collaboration: Open and honest communication is vital for a resilient team. It allows for the sharing of information, the identification of challenges, and the development of collaborative solutions.

Developing Problem-Solving Skills: Resilient teams are adept at problem-solving. Leaders should provide opportunities for teams to practice their problem-solving skills and create a toolkit of strategies for tackling challenges.

Embracing Diversity and Inclusion: A diverse team brings a range of perspectives and experiences that can enrich problem-solving and decision-making. By valuing diversity, leaders create more adaptable and better-equipped teams to navigate challenges.

Empowering Autonomy and Initiative: Resilient teams are empowered to take the initiative and make decisions within their area of responsibility. Leaders should encourage autonomy and provide opportunities for team members to develop their leadership skills.

Measuring Team Resilience:

While it's not always easy to quantify resilience, there are metrics and tools that can help leaders assess and track its progress:

Team Performance Metrics: Track team performance over time to identify areas of improvement and measure how effectively the team adapts to changes and overcomes challenges.

Employee Engagement Surveys: Regular surveys can gauge employee morale, satisfaction, and commitment to the team, providing insights into the team's overall well-being and resilience.

Feedback Mechanisms: Implement mechanisms for regular feedback, both formal and informal, to gather insights from team members about their experiences and identify areas for improvement.

Building a Legacy of Resilience:

Resilient teams are not built overnight. They are the product of ongoing effort, consistent leadership, and a commitment to continuous improvement. By understanding the key principles of resilience, leaders can empower their teams to overcome challenges and thrive in a rapidly changing world. Like those we've explored, their journeys will be a testament to the power of adaptability, collaboration, and a shared commitment to success.

Measuring Team Resilience

Resilience isn't just a desirable quality in leadership—it's a necessity. In today's rapidly changing world, organizations and teams constantly face unexpected challenges, market fluctuations, and technological disruptions. The ability to bounce back from adversity, adapt to new situations, and emerge stronger than before is crucial for sustained success.

But how do we measure this elusive concept of team resilience? While it might seem intangible at first, practical metrics and tools can provide valuable insights into a team's ability to withstand stress and thrive under pressure.

The Fundamentals of Measuring Resilience

Before diving into specific metrics, it's essential to understand the core components of team resilience. Think of resilience as a multifaceted construct, encompassing factors like:

Adaptability: The team's capacity to adjust to changing circumstances and embrace new approaches.

Problem-solving: The ability to identify challenges, analyze them effectively, and find creative solutions.

Communication and Collaboration: Clear and open communication channels that foster effective teamwork and mutual support.

Psychological Safety: A sense of trust and belonging that encourages team members to take risks, express their ideas, and learn from mistakes.

Emotional Regulation: The ability to manage stress, emotions, and pressure in a healthy and productive manner.

Motivation and Commitment: A shared sense of purpose and passion fuels the team's drive to succeed.

These components work together to create a resilient team capable of navigating complexities and achieving its goals.

Quantitative Metrics

While qualitative assessments are vital, quantitative metrics can provide valuable data points to track progress and measure resilience over time. Consider incorporating these metrics into your team's performance evaluation:

Turnaround Time: Measure how quickly a team can recover from setbacks or unexpected events. For example, track the time it takes to resolve a significant bug or recover from a data breach. A faster turnaround time indicates greater resilience.

Project Completion Rate: Monitor the team's success rate in completing projects on time and within budget. A high completion rate reflects a team's ability to overcome challenges and achieve its objectives.

Customer Satisfaction: Analyze customer feedback and satisfaction scores to gauge how well the team handles customer issues and delivers on expectations. High customer satisfaction demonstrates a team's ability to adapt to changing needs and provide excellent service.

Employee Engagement: Regularly assess employee morale, motivation, and overall engagement. A highly engaged team is more likely to be resilient, as employees feel valued and invested in the team's success.

Team Conflict Resolution Rate: Observe how effectively the team resolves internal conflicts and disagreements. A high conflict resolution rate indicates a team's capacity to manage differences and maintain positive working relation-ships.

Team Diversity and Inclusion: Measure the team's representation of diverse backgrounds, perspectives, and experiences. Teams with diverse perspectives are often more innovative and better equipped to handle complex challenges.

These quantitative metrics can provide valuable insights into the team's performance and highlight areas for improvement.

Qualitative Assessments

While quantitative metrics offer a snapshot of performance, qualitative assessments provide a deeper understanding of the underlying dynamics and processes contributing to resilience.

Team Surveys: Conduct regular surveys to gather feedback from team members on their perceived levels of resilience. Ask questions about their ability to adapt, handle pressure, and support one another.

Focus Groups and Interviews: Facilitate discussions and interviews with team members to explore their experiences, challenges, and strategies for managing stress and adversity. These qualitative insights can reveal valuable perspectives that quantitative data might miss.

Team Debriefing Sessions: After significant projects or challenging situations, hold debriefing sessions to analyze the team's performance, identify strengths and weaknesses, and discuss strategies for improvement.

Leadership Observations: Leaders should actively observe team dynamics and interactions to assess communication patterns, problem-solving approaches, and the team's ability to handle challenges.

Tools for Measuring Team Resilience

A range of tools can aid in assessing and enhancing team resilience. Consider utilizing these resources:

Resilience Assessment Tools: Numerous online and offline assessments can help teams assess their overall resilience levels and identify areas for improvement. These tools typically measure adaptability, problem-solving, communication, and stress management.

Personality and Behavioral Assessments: Tools like the Myers-Briggs Type Indicator (MBTI) or DISC assessment can help team members understand their strengths, weaknesses, and communication styles. This information can be used to build more cohesive teams and improve collaboration.

Emotional Intelligence Assessments: Emotional intelligence is crucial for building resilience. Assessments can help team members gauge their self-awareness, empathy, and relationship management skills.

Team-Building Activities: Team-building exercises and simulations can foster collaboration, communication, and trust among team members. These activities can also help the team learn to navigate challenges and work together effectively.

The Role of Technology

In today's digital age, technology is vital in enhancing team resilience. Numerous software solutions and platforms can support teams in various ways:

Project Management Tools: Tools like Asana, Trello, and Jira help teams track progress, manage tasks, and collaborate effectively on projects. By providing clarity and organization, these tools can improve efficiency and reduce stress levels.

Communication Platforms: Slack, Microsoft Teams, and Zoom facilitate seamless communication and collaboration among team members, regardless of location. Effective communication is critical for building resilience, as it allows for rapid information sharing, problem-solving, and support.

Data Analytics and Reporting Tools: Tools like Tableau and Power BI can help teams analyze performance data and identify patterns and trends. This data can inform decision-making, identify potential challenges, and help teams adapt to changing circumstances.

Learning Management Systems (LMS): Platforms like Moodle and Coursera provide access to online courses and resources that can help teams develop essential resilience skills, such as problem-solving, communication, and stress management.

Beyond Metrics and Tools: The Human Factor

While metrics and tools are valuable, it's crucial to recognize the human factor in building resilience. Fostering a positive and supportive team culture is essential:

Leadership Support: Leaders play a pivotal role in creating a resilient team environment. They should encourage open communication, provide clear expectations, and actively support team members through challenges.

Open Communication: Create an open and honest communication culture where team members feel comfortable sharing concerns, seeking feedback, and supporting one another.

Collaboration and Trust: Foster strong partnership and trust among team members. This enables them to work together effectively, share ideas openly, and rely on one another for support.

Continuous Learning: Encourage a culture of constant learning and development, where team members are empowered to expand their skills and knowledge. This adaptability is key to handling new challenges and emerging technologies.

Positive Work Environment: Cultivate a positive and supportive work environment where team members feel valued, respected, and encouraged to contribute their best efforts.

Measuring team resilience is not about simply ticking boxes or achieving arbitrary metrics. It's about understanding the fundamental elements contributing to a team's ability to withstand stress, adapt to change, and achieve its goals. By employing a combination of quantitative metrics, qualitative assessments, and robust tools, organizations can gain valuable insights into their teams' resilience and take actionable steps to enhance their ability to navigate the unpredictable landscape of the digital age. Building a resilient team requires a holistic approach encompassing data-driven insights and a commitment to fostering a supportive and dynamic work environment.

Chapter 4

Nurturing Creativity and Innovation

The Importance of Creativity in Leadership

In the ever-evolving landscape of modern business, where disruption and change are the only constants, the ability to think creatively is no longer just a desirable trait for leaders– it's an absolute necessity. Creativity is the engine that drives innovation, fuels problem-solving, and ultimately propels organizations forward. In this digitally driven era, where technology is constantly reshaping industries, businesses need leaders who can adapt to the changing landscape and actively shape it.

Imagine a company stuck in a rut, relying on the same old methods and strategies. Their products are stale, their customer base is shrinking, and their employees are uninspired. This is the picture of an organization that desperately needs a dose of creativity. Enter the visionary leader who dares to challenge the status quo, think outside the box, and explore new possibilities. This leader is fearless in experiments, embracing failure as a learning opportunity and inspiring their team to break free from traditional thinking.

Creativity in leadership isn't about simply conjuring up wild ideas out of thin air. It's about a systematic approach to problem-solving, a willingness to question assumptions and a relentless pursuit of better solutions. It's about fostering an environment where curiosity, experimentation, and collaboration thrive.

Think of Elon Musk at Tesla, the epitome of a visionary leader driven by an insatiable thirst for innovation. Musk's leadership style is marked by a relentless pursuit of cutting-edge technology and ambitious goals, from electric cars to reusable rockets. He challenges his team to think beyond conventional limits, constantly pushing the boundaries of what's possible. This relentless drive for innovation has transformed the automotive industry and inspired a generation of entrepreneurs and innovators.

Creativity in leadership is not just about product development; it's also about people. It's about understanding each team member's unique talents and perspectives and harnessing their collective creativity to solve complex problems. Leaders who foster a culture of creativity empower their team to think independently, express their ideas freely, and collaborate in a spirit of open dialogue and mutual respect.

A leader who values creativity embraces a variety of approaches to problem-solving. They encourage their team to explore unconventional ideas, to challenge the status quo, and to experiment with new solutions. This doesn't mean abandoning tried-and-true methods altogether. It's about balancing exploring new possibilities and leveraging existing knowledge and expertise.

Establishing a safe space for experimentation is a crucial element of fostering creativity in leadership. Leaders must create an environment where failure is not seen as a setback but as a valuable learning opportunity. This means encouraging teams to take calculated risks, embrace uncertainty, and learn from their mistakes.

Moreover, effective leaders understand that creativity is often fueled by diversity of thought. They actively seek out perspectives from different backgrounds, cultures, and experiences. This diversity of thought enriches problem-solving, leading to more innovative and effective solutions.

The benefits of fostering a creative leadership style are undeniable. Creative leaders are more likely to:

Drive innovation: Creative leaders constantly seek new ways to improve processes, products, and services. This leads to a culture of continuous innovation and a competitive advantage in the marketplace.

Solve complex problems: Creativity is essential for navigating the complexities of the modern business environment. Creative leaders can think outside the box to find innovative solutions to complex challenges.

Motivate and engage employees: When employees feel empowered to be creative, they are more likely to be involved and motivated. This leads to higher levels of productivity and job satisfaction.

Build stronger relationships: Creativity often involves collaboration and teamwork. Creative leaders foster a collaborative environment that strengthens relationships among team members.

Increase adaptability: In today's fast-paced world, adaptability is key to success. Creative leaders are better equipped to adapt to changing circumstances and to embrace new challenges.

The journey towards fostering creativity in leadership can be challenging. There will be roadblocks, moments of uncertainty, and setbacks along the way. However, with a commitment to experimentation, a willingness to challenge the status quo, and a focus on building a culture of innovation, leaders can unlock the transformative power of creativity and drive their organizations to new heights of success.

Creating a Culture of Innovation

Imagine a bustling marketplace where ideas are traded like precious commodities. This is the environment thriving companies cultivate – where creativity is celebrated, and innovation is the lifeblood. But how do you, as a leader, create this vibrant ecosystem within your organization? It's not just about throwing a few brainstorming sessions and calling it a day. Nurturing a culture of innovation requires a shift in mindset and a deliberate approach to foster an environment where everyone feels empowered to contribute, experiment, and push boundaries.

This isn't just about encouraging employees to create new product features or marketing campaigns; it's about creating a culture where everyone feels valued, heard, and supported in their pursuit of creative solutions. It's about fostering a safe space for risks and failures, where these are seen not as setbacks but as stepping stones to greater success.

Think of it like a garden. You don't simply plant seeds and expect them to bloom. You nurture the soil, provide sunlight and water, and weed out any obstacles hindering their growth. Similarly, cultivating a culture of innovation requires constant care and attention.

Let's start with **empowerment**. Imagine a world where employees can freely explore their ideas without fear of judgment or rejection. This is the foundation of a culture of innovation. It begins by actively listening to your team's suggestions, regardless of how outlandish they might seem at first. A seemingly crazy idea might hold the key to unlocking a breakthrough.

Remember, **creativity thrives in a space of trust and respect**. Leaders who foster a culture of open communication and transparency create a space where ideas can flourish. Encourage feedback, both positive and constructive. This creates a collaborative environment where ideas are challenged, refined, and strengthened.

Diversity is another key ingredient. Bringing together individuals with different perspectives, experiences, and expertise can spark unexpected combinations of ideas. This cross-pollination of thoughts can lead to innovative solutions that no individual might have conceived alone.

Don't underestimate the power of **playfulness**. Encourage your team to approach challenges with curiosity and experiment with different approaches. Breaking free from rigid thinking can lead to unexpected breakthroughs. Organize creative workshops and hackathons or dedicate some work time to exploring new ideas.

Rewards and recognition are also vital. Celebrate successes, big and small. Publicly acknowledge and reward innovative solutions, even if they don't directly translate into a groundbreaking product or service. This reinforces that creativity is valued and contributes to a positive innovation cycle.

Remember, innovation is only sometimes about creating something entirely new. Often, it's about finding new ways to improve existing processes or products. Encourage your team to look for inefficiencies and find innovative ways to streamline operations. This can lead to significant gains in productivity and efficiency.

The path to a culture of innovation is an ongoing journey, not a destination. It requires continuous effort, open communication, and a willingness to embrace change. Don't be afraid to experiment, fail, learn, and iterate. The more you cultivate a culture of innovation, the more your team will be inspired to push boundaries and unlock their full creative potential.

Let's take a look at some real-world examples of companies that have successfully fostered a culture of innovation:

Google's 20% Time: This initiative encourages employees to spend 20% of their work time on personal projects they're passionate about. This has resulted in groundbreaking products like Gmail and Google Maps.

Netflix's Freedom & Responsibility Culture: Netflix empowers employees to make decisions and work autonomously. This fosters a culture of experimentation and innovation, allowing employees to take ownership of their work and pursue creative solutions.

Tesla's Innovation through Design: Tesla focuses on creating products that are not only technologically advanced but also aesthetically pleasing. This approach has led to vehicles that are considered both innovative and desirable.

These examples demonstrate that nurturing a culture of innovation is not just a theoretical concept but a practical approach yielding tangible results. By incorporating the above principles, you can create an environment where creativity flourishes and innovation drives success.

Don't forget the human element: Innovation doesn't happen in a vacuum. It's driven by the passion, creativity, and ingenuity of the people who contribute to your organization. Create a workplace where everyone feels valued, supported, and inspired to make a difference. This is the key to unlocking your team's full potential and building a culture of innovation that will lead your organization to new heights.

Techniques for Creative Thinking

Creativity is the lifeblood of innovation, and in the rapidly evolving world of business, it's an essential skill for leaders.

A leader who can inspire and guide their team to think outside the box, challenge the status quo, and come up with fresh solutions is invaluable. But creativity isn't a magical ability; it's a muscle that needs to be exercised and nurtured.

Think of it like this: you wouldn't expect to run a marathon without training. The same goes for creative thinking. It requires conscious effort, deliberate practice, and a willingness to embrace the unexpected.

Unlocking Your Creative Potential

Let's explore some techniques and exercises that can help you tap into your creative potential:

Brainstorming: This classic technique is a great starting point for generating ideas. Gather a team, set a timer, and let the ideas flow. Don't censor yourself or worry about practicality at this stage. The goal is to get as many ideas on the table as possible.

Mind Mapping: Mind mapping is a visual brainstorming technique that helps you explore different branches of an idea. Start with a central topic and then branch into related ideas, connecting them with lines and arrows. This can help you see connections and patterns you might have yet to notice.

SCAMPER: SCAMPER is a technique that uses a series of questions to spark new ideas by modifying existing ones. The acronym stands for:

Substitute: Can you replace any component of the idea?
Combine: Can you merge two or more ideas?
Adapt: Can you adjust the idea to fit a different situation?
Modify: Can you change any feature of the concept?
Put to other uses: Can you use the idea differently?
Eliminate: Can you remove any part of the idea?
Reverse: Can you turn the idea around?

Lateral Thinking: The problem-solving approach encourages you to think outside the box and challenge assumptions. It involves looking for new perspectives, questioning the obvious, and considering alternative solutions.

The "What If" Game: Ask yourself "What if" questions to stimulate creative thinking. This could involve exploring different scenarios, challenging existing beliefs, or imagining alternative outcomes.

Role-playing: Putting yourself in someone else's shoes can help you see things from a different perspective. Try role-playing as a customer, competitor, or future version of yourself. This can help you identify new opportunities or challenges you might have overlooked.

Analogies and Metaphors: Drawing comparisons between different concepts can help you generate new ideas. For example, you might compare a business challenge to a puzzle or a problem to a game.

Visualizing: Imagery can be a powerful tool for creative thinking. Close your eyes and picture the desired outcome or the ideal solution to a problem. This can help you tap into your subconscious mind and come up with innovative ideas.

Creative Time: Dedicate specific time slots for innovative thinking. This could be a daily ritual, a weekly meeting, or a weekend getaway. Creating a dedicated space and time for creative brainstorming can help you focus and generate more ideas.

Experiment and Play: Be bold and experiment with different ideas, even if they seem unconventional. The best ideas often come from unexpected sources. Encourage a playful and experimental approach to problem-solving.

Building a Culture of Creativity

Nurturing a culture of creativity within your team is crucial for continuous innovation. Here are some strategies to foster a creative environment:

Encourage Experimentation: Create a culture where it's okay to try new things, fail, and learn from those failures. Encourage team members to take risks and experiment with new ideas.

Embrace Diversity: A diverse team brings many different perspectives and experiences. Encourage collaboration between individuals with different backgrounds and expertise.

Provide Freedom and Autonomy: Give your team the freedom to explore their ideas and the autonomy to make decisions within their areas of responsibility.

Celebrate Successes and Failures: Recognize and celebrate both successes and failures. Acknowledge that learning from setbacks is an integral part of the creative process.

Foster Curiosity: Encourage team members to ask questions, challenge assumptions, and seek out new information.

Provide Support and Resources: Ensure your team has access to the tools, resources, and support they need to bring their creative ideas to life. This might include access to technology, mentorship, or training opportunities.

Open Communication: Create an environment where team members feel comfortable sharing their ideas openly and honestly without fear of judgment.

Promote Collaboration: Encourage team members to collaborate, share ideas, and build upon each other's thoughts. This can lead to cross-pollination of ideas and a more innovative outcome.

Embrace the Unexpected: Don't be afraid of surprises or unexpected results. Often, the most innovative ideas emerge from unexpected places.

Continuous Learning: Encourage a culture of constant learning and development. Provide opportunities for team members to expand their knowledge and skills, which can lead to new insights and creative solutions.

Balancing Creativity with Practicality

While creativity is essential, it's crucial to balance it with practicality. You want to generate a manageable number of brilliant ideas that are possible and practical to implement.

Here's how to ensure your team's creativity is grounded in reality:

Define Clear Goals: Before embarking on a creative journey, ensure you have clear goals and objectives. This will help you stay focused and ensure the ideas generated are relevant to your needs.

Prioritize Ideas: Once you have a collection of ideas, prioritize them based on their potential impact, feasibility, and alignment with your goals.

Test and Iterate: Be bold, test your ideas, and iterate on them based on the feedback you receive. This helps ensure that your creative solutions are innovative and viable.

Seek Feedback: Get feedback from stakeholders, customers, and experts in the field. This can help you identify potential flaws or limitations in your ideas and make necessary adjustments.

Embrace Agile Development: Employ agile methodologies to develop and refine your creative solutions iteratively. This allows for flexibility and adaptability as you progress.

Recognizing and Rewarding Innovation

Recognizing and rewarding innovation is crucial to fostering a culture of creativity. Make sure your team feels valued and appreciated for their efforts:

Celebrate Successes: Publicly acknowledge and celebrate innovative achievements. Highlight the contributions of individuals and teams that have significantly contributed to your organization's creative endeavors.

Offer Recognition: Use incentives and rewards to recognize creative breakthroughs. This could include financial bonuses, promotions, or a public thank you.

Provide Growth Opportunities: Invest in your team members' professional development. Offer them opportunities to learn new skills, expand their knowledge, and explore new areas of interest.

Create a Culture of Feedback: Encourage open and constructive feedback. Create a safe space for team members to share their thoughts and ideas without fear of judgment.

Lead by Example: As a leader, champion creativity and innovation. Embrace new ideas, experiment with new approaches, and encourage your team to do the same.

Remember, a culture of creativity is not built overnight. It requires consistent effort, commitment, and a willingness to embrace change. By fostering a supportive and stimulating environment, you can unleash your team's creative potential and unlock a world of possibilities.

Balancing Creativity with Practicality

Creativity is the lifeblood of innovation, but it's not enough to have a brilliant idea. Translating that spark into a practical and implementable solution is the real challenge. It's like having a beautiful painting, but without a canvas or paint, it remains a mere concept, never to be realized. So, how do you balance the free-flowing energy of creativity with the grounded nature of practicality?

The key lies in creating a structured environment where ideas can flourish and be guided and refined. Imagine a garden—you plant seeds, nurture them with water and sunlight, and prune away the weeds to ensure healthy growth. Similarly, in the business realm, you must provide a fertile ground for ideas to germinate, offering the resources and support necessary to blossom while pruning away the impractical and unviable ones.

Here's a framework for striking this delicate balance:

1 – The Ideation Stage: Unleashing the Creative Flow

Embrace Diversity: Encourage a variety of perspectives. Teams composed of individuals with diverse backgrounds, experiences, and thought processes are more likely to generate a broader range of ideas. A blend of technical expertise, creative thinking, and strategic vision can lead to innovative solutions. Think of a brainstorming session– the more diverse the participants, the richer the tapestry of ideas.

Create a Safe Space: Foster a culture that celebrates experimentation and risk-taking. The fear of failure can stifle creativity. Encourage employees to share their ideas, even if they seem unconventional or offbeat.

Remember, it's in the unexpected corners that ground-breaking ideas often emerge.

Embrace Playfulness: Encourage a playful approach to problem-solving. Games, challenges, and informal workshops can stimulate creative thinking. Don't be afraid to step outside the box. Remember, the most innovative solutions often come from unexpected places. Think of companies like Google, whose "20% time" policy encourages employees to pursue their projects. This playful approach has led to developing groundbreaking products like Gmail and Google Maps.

2 - The Evaluation Stage: Sorting the Wheat from the Chaff

Define Your Objectives: Be crystal clear about your goals. What problem are you trying to solve? What are your key performance indicators (KPIs)? Having a clear vision and measurable targets will help you assess the practicality of ideas. Without a clear objective, your creative energy might be dispersed like a scattering of stars, unable to create a coherent constellation.

Conduct Feasibility Analysis: Before investing significant resources, determine if the idea is technically feasible, financially viable, and aligns with your overall strategy. A feasibility analysis involves a deep dive into an idea's practical aspects, assessing its potential for success. This involves market research, financial projections, and technical assessments. It's like building a bridge—you need to carefully analyze the terrain, the materials, and the forces that will act upon it.

Seek Constructive Feedback: Don't shy away from critique. Invite feedback from diverse stakeholders, such as colleagues, customers, and subject matter experts. This will help identify potential roadblocks and refine the idea.

Remember, constructive criticism is a gift that can help you polish your ideas to their full potential. It's like having a sculptor chiseling away at a block of marble to reveal the masterpiece within.

3 - The Implementation Stage: From Idea to Reality

Break Down the Idea: Divide the idea into smaller, manageable steps. This will make the implementation process more manageable and achievable. Think of a complex puzzle – you wouldn't try to assemble it all at once, but rather piece by piece, working towards a clear solution.

Assign Roles and Responsibilities: Clearly define who is responsible for what. This ensures accountability and eliminates confusion during the execution phase. It's like a symphony orchestra – each musician plays their assigned part, contributing to the harmonious whole.

Iterate and Adapt: Be bold and change course if needed. Flexibility is crucial in a dynamic business environment. Constant iteration and adaptation are essential to navigating the ever-changing landscape of business.

Think of a ship sailing through a stormy sea – it must adjust its course and navigate the waves to stay afloat.

Practical Examples: A Real-World Perspective

Let's look at a few practical examples of how companies have balanced creativity with practicality:

Airbnb: Airbnb's initial idea – to connect travelers with spare rooms – was born out of a personal need. However, they carefully analyzed the market, validated the concept, and built a platform that addressed the needs of both hosts and guests. Their focus on user experience, data-driven decision-making, and continuous iteration have fueled their phenomenal growth.

Tesla: Elon Musk's vision of electric vehicles was not entirely new, but his ability to blend cutting-edge technology, innovative design, and a compelling brand narrative has transformed the industry. Tesla's success lies in its ability to constantly push boundaries while remaining grounded in practical considerations—ensuring its cars are safe, reliable, and meet consumer demands.

Netflix: Netflix didn't invent streaming, but it recognized its potential and built a platform that revolutionized entertainment consumption. Their data-driven approach to content creation, personalized recommendations, and constant experimentation have allowed them to stay ahead of the curve. Netflix is a testament to the power of embracing change and adapting to the evolving demands of the market.

Nurturing creativity and innovation requires a delicate balance – a delicate dance between the artistic expression of ideas and the practical application of those ideas. It's about striking the right chord between imagination and execution, inspiration and implementation. By following the steps outlined above, you can create an environment that welcomes creativity and guides it towards actionable solutions. Remember, it's not about suppressing creativity but channeling it to yield tangible results, turning those flashes of brilliance into practical and impactful outcomes. The true mark of a successful leader is not simply having great ideas but the ability to bring those ideas to life, turning them into a reality that benefits everyone. So, go forth and unleash your inner innovator, armed with the spark of creativity and the compass of practicality.

Recognizing and Rewarding Innovation

Imagine a team where every member feels empowered to contribute their unique ideas, creative sparks fly, and innovation is encouraged and celebrated. This is the kind of environment that fosters a culture of growth, and it's something that every leader should aspire to create.

But how do you make this happen? How do you cultivate a space where innovation thrives, and every team member feels valued for their creative contributions?

The answer lies in recognizing and rewarding innovation. It's not just about offering financial incentives; it's about fostering a culture where creativity is truly valued.

Think of it this way: imagine a company where the CEO, upon hearing a brilliant idea from a junior employee, shrugs and says, "That's nice, but we're not doing that." What message does that send? It sends a message that innovation isn't valued, that creativity is discouraged, and that the status quo is king.

On the other hand, imagine a company where the CEO jumps at the opportunity to explore that same idea, eagerly seeking feedback from the team and brainstorming ways to implement it. This company is signaling to its employees that their ideas are valuable, that their creativity is appreciated, and that they are empowered to contribute to the company's success.

Recognizing and rewarding innovation is more than just a nice gesture; it's a powerful tool for building a high-performing team, attracting and retaining top talent, and driving growth. Here's how it works:

Boosting Morale and Engagement: When employees feel valued and recognized for their creative contributions, their morale and engagement skyrocket. They are more likely to be motivated, invested in their work, and more eager to contribute.

Attracting and Retaining Talent: In today's competitive job market, talented individuals are drawn to companies that value innovation and provide opportunities for professional growth. Creating a culture where innovation is recognized and rewarded makes your company a magnet for the best and brightest minds.

Driving Innovation and Growth: When employees feel empowered to share their ideas and know that their contributions are valued, they are more likely to devise innovative solutions to challenges. This, in turn, drives the company's growth and success.

Creating a Culture of Continuous Learning: When employees see their colleagues being recognized for their creative efforts, it encourages them to think outside the box and push their boundaries. This fosters a continuous learning and development culture where everyone constantly strives to improve and innovate.

Creating a Strong Team Identity: When team members feel like their ideas are valued and their contributions are making a difference, they strengthen their identity and foster a sense of shared purpose. This, in turn, creates a more cohesive and effective team that can better overcome challenges and achieve goals.

Rewarding Innovation Beyond Financial Incentives: While financial incentives can be a part of recognizing innovative efforts, they shouldn't be the only form of reward. Here are some additional ways to show your team that their creativity is valued:

Public Recognition: Acknowledge and praise innovative ideas in team meetings, company newsletters, or social media. This public recognition can boost employee morale and encourage others to embrace creativity.

Mentorship and Training: Offer opportunities for mentorship and training in areas related to innovation and creative problem-solving. This can help employees develop their skills and unleash their full potential.

Opportunities for Growth: Provide opportunities for employees to take on new challenges and projects that allow them to apply their innovative thinking. This can be leading new initiatives, participating in cross-functional teams, or developing new products and services.

Flexible Work Arrangements: Offer flexible work arrangements, such as remote work options or flexible schedules, to allow employees more time and freedom to explore their creative ideas.

Encouraging Brainstorming and Collaboration: Create opportunities for team members to brainstorm and share ideas. This can be done through regular team meetings, dedicated innovation sessions, or online platforms where employees can share their thoughts and feedback.

Celebrate Failures: It's important to remember that not all innovative ideas will be successful. Create a culture where failure is okay, and failures are seen as learning opportunities.

Embrace a Culture of Experimentation: Encourage a culture that embraces experimentation. Allow team members to try out new ideas and approaches, even if they don't always succeed. This will help foster a more innovative mindset and encourage risk-taking.

A Case Study in Innovation Recognition:

Let's look at a real-world example of a company that has successfully implemented a culture of innovation recognition:

Google is renowned for its creative culture. They have a long history of rewarding innovative ideas and providing opportunities for employees to grow and develop their skills.

Google's "20% Time" policy allows employees to spend 20% of their time working on personal projects. This policy has resulted in some of the company's most successful products, including Gmail and Google Maps. It encourages employees to explore their passions and develop new ideas, ultimately leading to a culture of continuous innovation.

In addition to the "20% Time" policy, Google has a robust innovation program called "Google Ventures," which invests in and supports promising startups. This program provides funding, mentorship, and other resources to help these startups succeed, further fostering a culture of innovation within the Google ecosystem.

Google's approach to innovation recognition has been instrumental in its success. By creating a culture where innovation is celebrated and rewarded, the company has attracted and retained some of the world's most talented individuals, driven the development of groundbreaking products, and ultimately, transformed how we use technology.

Recognizing and rewarding innovation is crucial for any company that wants to thrive in the digital age. By creating a culture where creative thinking is valued and encouraged, you will not only attract and retain top talent but also unlock your team's full potential, driving innovation and growth in the process.

Remember, it's not just about financial rewards; it's about creating an environment where every team member feels empowered to contribute their unique ideas and where their creativity is celebrated. By embracing this mindset, you'll be on your way to building a truly innovative and successful organization.

Chapter 5

Insights from Industry Leaders

Lessons from Tech Giants

In modern business, where innovation and disruption are the driving forces, the leadership lessons learned from tech giants like Google and Apple hold profound significance; these companies have revolutionized their respective industries and established unique leadership cultures that have served as inspiration and benchmarks for countless organizations worldwide.

Google's "Data-Driven" Approach to Leadership:

Google has built a reputation for its innovative products and services, fueled by a data-driven approach to decision-making. This approach extends to its leadership philosophy as well. At Google, data isn't just a tool; it's a guiding principle. Leaders at Google are encouraged to rely on data insights to understand the needs of their teams, track progress toward goals, and make informed decisions. This data-driven approach fosters a culture of accountability, where every decision is backed by evidence and analysis.

Key Takeaways from Google's Leadership:

Embrace Experimentation: Google encourages a culture of experimentation, where employees are free to explore new ideas and test them in a safe environment. The company's "Fail Fast" philosophy encourages employees to embrace failure as a learning opportunity, fostering a culture of continuous improvement.

Empowerment and Autonomy: Google believes in empowering its employees to make decisions and take ownership of their work. This autonomy extends to all levels of the organization, creating a sense of ownership and responsibility.

Focus on Impact: Google prioritizes projects and initiatives that have a tangible impact on users and the broader community. This focus on impact ensures that all efforts are aligned with the company's mission and values.

Transparency and Communication: Google emphasizes open and transparent communication within teams and the organization. This promotes collaboration and ensures everyone is aligned on goals and priorities.

Apple's "Focus on Design and User Experience" Leadership:

Apple, known for its sleek and intuitive products, has a leadership culture that strongly emphasizes design and user experience. Apple's leaders prioritize creating products that solve problems and delight users.

This focus on design extends to everything from product development to the company's overall brand identity.

Key Takeaways from Apple's Leadership:

Passion for Excellence: Apple's leadership team is driven by a passion for excellence in everything they do. This passion translates into a relentless pursuit of quality and innovation.

Customer-Centric Approach: Apple's leaders are obsessed with understanding the needs and desires of their customers.

This customer-centric approach guides everything from product development to marketing and customer support.

Attention to Detail: Apple's leaders pay meticulous attention to detail, ensuring that every aspect of their products and services is polished and refined. This attention to detail is evident in everything from product design to packaging and marketing materials.

Strong Brand Identity: Apple has carefully cultivated a strong and consistent brand identity that resonates with its target audience. This brand identity is reflected in everything from product design to marketing campaigns and retail stores.

The Intersection of Google and Apple's Leadership:

While Google and Apple have different approaches to leadership, they both share specific fundamental values that contribute to their success:

Innovation: Both Google and Apple are known for their commitment to innovation, constantly pushing the boundaries of technology and design. This commitment to innovation is driven by a willingness to experiment, embrace change, and think outside the box.

Customer Focus: Both companies prioritize customer satisfaction and are driven by a deep understanding of their customers' needs and desires. This customer focus is reflected in their product development, marketing, and customer support strategies.

Strong Culture: Both Google and Apple have cultivated strong and distinctive company cultures that attract and retain top talent. These cultures are characterized by values like collaboration, innovation, and a passion for what they do.

Lessons for Modern Leaders:

The leadership lessons from Google and Apple apply to leaders across industries and organization sizes.

Here are some key takeaways for modern leaders:

Embrace Data-Driven Decision Making: Use data to inform your decisions and make informed choices based on evidence.

Foster a Culture of Innovation: Encourage experimentation, embrace failure as a learning opportunity, and create an environment where new ideas can flourish.

Empower Your Teams: Give your employees the autonomy and responsibility to make decisions and own their work.

Focus on Impact: Ensure that your efforts are aligned with your organization's mission and have a tangible impact on your customers and the wider community.

Cultivate a Strong Brand Identity: Define your organization's values, mission, and vision, and communicate them effectively to your employees, customers, and stakeholders.

Applying Tech Giant Lessons to Your Organization:

To effectively apply the leadership lessons from tech giants like Google and Apple to your organization, you need to:

Identify Your Unique Strengths: What are your company's core values and differentiators? Leverage your strengths to create a unique and compelling leadership culture.

Tailor Strategies to Your Context: Not every approach will work for every organization. Adapt the lessons from tech giants to your specific industry, size, and context.

Continuously Learn and Adapt: The business landscape is constantly evolving. Stay informed about industry trends, best practices, and emerging technologies to adapt your leadership style and strategies accordingly.

The Future of Leadership:

As technology evolves at an unprecedented pace, the role of leadership will continue to transform. Leaders who embrace innovation, adaptability, and a human-centric approach will be best equipped to navigate the challenges and opportunities of the future. By drawing inspiration from tech giants like Google and Apple, modern leaders can develop the skills and mindsets needed to thrive in the digital age and lead their organizations to success.

The leadership lessons learned from tech giants like Google and Apple offer valuable insights into building a thriving organization. By embracing their data-driven approach, customer-centric focus, and commitment to innovation, modern leaders can create a culture that fosters creativity, empowers employees, and drives impactful results. In today's fast-paced and technology-driven world, these lessons provide a roadmap for navigating the complexities of modern leadership and leading with purpose and passion. The journey of leadership is ongoing and filled with challenges and rewards. By learning from the successes and failures of others, we can gain valuable insights that empower us to become more effective and impactful leaders, inspiring our teams to achieve their full potential and drive positive change in the world.

Innovative Startups and Their Leaders

The world of startups is a whirlwind of energy, innovation, and relentless hustle. From Silicon Valley to Bangalore, these young companies are disrupting industries and shaping the future. But behind the cutting-edge technology and ambitious goals, there are extraordinary leaders who drive their ventures to success. These leaders are often unconventional, bold, and fiercely passionate about their vision. They're not afraid to take risks, push boundaries, and inspire their teams to achieve the seemingly impossible.

Let's dive into the stories of some innovative startups and their inspiring leaders, uncovering the principles and practices that have fueled their remarkable journeys:

The Visionary: Elon Musk at Tesla and SpaceX: Elon Musk, the name evokes a sense of awe and wonder. He's not just a CEO; he's a visionary who dares to dream big and relentlessly pursue those dreams. His ventures, Tesla and SpaceX, have revolutionized electric vehicles and space exploration.

Musk's leadership style is characterized by an intense focus on innovation, an unwavering commitment to pushing the limits of technology, and a relentless drive for results. He sets ambitious goals and challenges his teams to reach for the stars. He fosters a culture of continuous improvement, always seeking to refine processes and break new ground. Musk's relentless pursuit of innovation and his willingness to challenge the status quo inspire not only his employees but millions worldwide.

The Culture Builder: Reed Hastings at Netflix: Netflix has become synonymous with streaming entertainment, and its rise to dominance is a testament to Reed Hastings's visionary leadership. Hastings recognized the potential of online video streaming and built a company that disrupted the traditional television industry. Beyond his business acumen, Hastings is renowned for his forward-thinking approach to management. He champions employee autonomy and flexibility, emphasizing trust and ownership over rigid hierarchies. Netflix has embraced remote work and created a culture of innovation and experimentation, allowing its employees to work independently and pursue their passions. Hastings believes in investing in his employees and allowing them to explore new ideas and take risks. This approach has resulted in a highly engaged and productive workforce constantly pushing the entertainment industry's boundaries.

The Data-Driven Leader: Brian Chesky at Airbnb: Airbnb's success story is a testament to the power of a simple but disruptive idea: connecting travelers with people willing to share their homes. Airbnb's co-founder and CEO Brian Chesky has nurtured a culture of data-driven decision-making and innovation. Chesky's leadership style is characterized by his ability to understand his users' needs and translate that understanding into practical solutions. He uses data to guide the company's growth, constantly iterating and refining its offerings based on user feedback. Chesky's leadership has led to a platform that has empowered millions of people to travel the world and experience different cultures while fostering a sense of community and belonging.

The Agile Innovator: Evan Spiegel at Snapchat:
With its ephemeral messaging and unique features, Snapchat has become a cultural phenomenon, capturing the attention of a generation. Evan Spiegel, the company's co-founder and CEO, masters innovation and agility. Spiegel's leadership is characterized by his focus on understanding young users' evolving needs and preferences. He's constantly experimenting with new features and technologies, embracing a culture of rapid prototyping and iteration. Spiegel's willingness to take risks and adapt to the changing landscape of social media has kept Snapchat at the forefront of innovation, proving that success in the digital age requires a dynamic and agile approach.

These are just a few examples of the many inspiring leaders shaping the startup landscape. Their stories offer valuable insights into the principles and practices that drive success in the digital age. They demonstrate the importance of vision, innovation, agility, and a relentless focus on customer needs. These leaders are not just building businesses; they're building the future. They are pushing boundaries, challenging conventions, and inspiring generations to come.

What can we learn from these startup leaders?

Embrace a Growth Mindset: Successful startup leaders possess a growth mindset, constantly seeking to learn and adapt. They're not afraid to experiment, fail, and learn from their mistakes. They view challenges as opportunities for growth and improvement.

Foster a Culture of Innovation: Creating a culture of innovation is paramount in the fast-paced world of startups. Leaders must encourage their teams to think outside the box, challenge the status quo, and embrace new ideas. They need to provide the space and resources for experimentation and creative problem-solving.

Prioritize Customer Needs: Startup success is ultimately driven by meeting customers' needs. Leaders must deeply understand their target audience and constantly seek ways to improve their products and services.

Lead with Passion and Purpose: Successful startup leaders are passionate about their vision and purpose. They are not driven solely by profit; they believe in the impact their companies can make on the world. They are driven by a desire to make a difference and leave a lasting legacy.

Embrace Change and Adaptability: The startup landscape is constantly evolving. Leaders must be adaptable and willing to change course when necessary. They need to pivot quickly and respond to emerging trends and opportunities.

Build Strong Teams: The best startup leaders know that success is a team effort. They build strong, diverse teams with complementary skills and perspectives. They prioritize collaboration, communication, and trust.

The journey of a startup is rarely smooth. There will be challenges, setbacks, and moments of doubt. However, the leaders who can navigate these obstacles, learn from their mistakes and adapt to changing circumstances are the ones who are most likely to succeed. By embracing the principles and practices of these innovative leaders, we can all learn to lead with vision, passion, and purpose and contribute to building a brighter future.

The Role of Mentorship in Leadership

In the tapestry of professional development, mentorship emerges as a vibrant thread, weaving together experiences, knowledge, and guidance that shape the careers of industry leaders. It's not just about receiving advice; it's about forging a relationship built on trust, respect, and a shared commitment to growth. Mentorship serves as a catalyst for unlocking potential, expanding horizons, and navigating the complexities of the business world.

Think of mentorship as a compass, guiding individuals through challenges and opportunities.

Mentors provide a unique perspective, drawing on their trials and triumphs to offer valuable insights and support. They act as sounding boards, offering a safe space to explore ideas, articulate challenges, and gain clarity on the path forward. This process of reflection and feedback is crucial for self-awareness and continuous improvement.

Let's take a closer look at how mentorship has shaped the careers of some of the most influential leaders in our time:

Elon Musk, the Visionary Entrepreneur

Elon Musk, the visionary behind Tesla and SpaceX, credits his mentors for shaping his entrepreneurial spirit. He learned from Peter Thiel, a renowned venture capitalist, the importance of challenging assumptions and taking bold risks. Thiel's mentorship gave Musk the confidence to pursue his ambitious ventures, pushing the boundaries of innovation in electric vehicles and space exploration.

Indra Nooyi, the Trailblazing CEO

Indra Nooyi, the former CEO of PepsiCo, attributes her success to the mentors who believed in her potential and challenged her to reach greater heights. She credits her mentors for instilling in her the importance of inclusivity, building strong teams, and fostering a culture of collaboration. Nooyi's leadership journey was paved by the unwavering support and guidance she received from mentors who encouraged her to break through barriers and achieve unprecedented heights.

Satya Nadella, the Transformative Leader

Satya Nadella, the CEO of Microsoft, acknowledges the transformative impact of mentorship on his leadership style. He learned from Bill Gates, the co-founder of Microsoft, the importance of empowering employees, fostering a culture of innovation, and embracing the power of technology.

Nadella's journey from technical leader to CEO is a testament to the power of mentorship in shaping a transformative leader.

The Importance of Mentorship in Leadership

The examples of Musk, Nooyi, and Nadella illustrate a common thread: mentorship plays a pivotal role in developing successful leaders. Mentorship fosters a sense of purpose, provides guidance during challenging times, and instills the confidence to navigate the ever-evolving landscape of the business world.

Here are some of the key benefits of mentorship for aspiring leaders:

Personal Growth: Mentorship provides a safe space for self-reflection, allowing individuals to identify their strengths, weaknesses, and areas for improvement. Mentors offer constructive feedback, helping individuals better understand their leadership potential.

Skill Development: Mentors share their expertise and experience, guiding individuals to hone their skills and acquire new knowledge. From strategic thinking to effective communication, mentorship provides a structured framework for skill development.

Career Guidance: Mentors provide valuable insights into career paths, industry trends, and potential opportunities. They offer advice on navigating career transitions and making strategic choices.

Network Expansion: Mentors often introduce their mentees to their professional network, creating valuable connections and expanding career horizons. This network can provide support, inspiration, and potential opportunities.

Building Confidence: Mentorship fosters a belief in one's abilities, encouraging individuals to step outside their comfort zones and take on new challenges. Mentors provide a supportive environment, allowing individuals to experiment, learn from their mistakes, and build confidence in their leadership capabilities.

Navigating the Mentorship Journey

The mentorship journey is a two-way street, demanding a commitment from both mentor and mentee. Here are some key considerations for navigating this relationship successfully:

Finding the Right Mentor: It's crucial to find a mentor who aligns with your career aspirations, possesses the experience you seek, and shares your values. Look for mentors willing to invest time and effort in your development.

Clear Communication: Establish clear expectations and goals for the mentorship relationship. Discuss the frequency of meetings, the topics you wish to explore, and the level of involvement you desire from your mentor.

Active Listening: Pay attention to your mentor's advice, ask clarifying questions, and demonstrate your eagerness to learn. Effective communication fosters trust and ensures you receive the most value from the mentorship experience.

Taking the initiative: Be bold, ask questions, seek guidance, and take the initiative in your development. Your commitment and willingness to learn will create a more fulfilling mentorship experience.

Building a Lasting Relationship: Mentorship is not a one-time event; it's a long-term relationship. Nurture your connection with your mentor, seek their advice, and express gratitude for their support.

Mentorship is a powerful force in shaping leaders and fostering professional growth. It's a journey of learning, discovery, and transformation. By embracing the transformative power of mentorship, individuals can unlock their leadership potential and make a meaningful impact in their organizations and the world.

Adapting to Market Changes

Adapting to market changes is a hallmark of successful leadership, especially in the rapidly evolving digital age. Leaders who embrace agility and nimbleness are the ones who thrive in the face of disruption and uncertainty.

We've seen countless examples of companies and their leaders navigating significant market shifts with remarkable success.

Take, for instance, the story of Netflix. In the early 2000s, Netflix focused on DVD rentals by mail. However, the rise of streaming services like YouTube and Hulu and the advent of high-speed internet presented a significant challenge to Netflix's business model.

Instead of clinging to the past, Netflix's leadership team made a bold decision: they embraced the streaming revolution. They invested heavily in developing their streaming platform, transitioned their business model, and ultimately became the undisputed king of online streaming.

This adaptability allowed them to survive and thrive in a rapidly changing market.

Another inspiring example is the rise of Amazon. From humble beginnings as an online bookseller, Amazon, under Jeff Bezos's leadership, has transformed itself into a behemoth encompassing e-commerce, cloud computing, digital streaming, and more. Amazon's success story is a testament to its ability to anticipate and respond to market trends, constantly innovating and expanding its reach. Bezos's vision and his leadership team's ability to adapt to changing customer needs have propelled Amazon to become one of the most valuable companies in the world.

The ability to adapt is not limited to tech giants. Consider the case of Patagonia, a company known for its commitment to sustainability and environmental activism. Patagonia has positioned itself as a leader in responsible business practices in a world increasingly concerned about climate change and its impact. They have actively advocated for policies that protect the environment, challenged industry standards, and even donated millions to environmental causes. By aligning its business with societal values, Patagonia has carved a unique niche and attracted a loyal customer base that resonates with its ethical stance.

These are just a few examples of how leaders have adapted to market changes and achieved remarkable success. But it can be challenging; adapting to new trends and challenges often requires courage, creativity, and a willingness to embrace uncertainty. It also demands a keen understanding of the market, a commitment to continuous learning, and the ability to inspire and motivate your team to embrace change.

Here are some key takeaways from industry leaders who have successfully navigated significant market shifts:

Embrace the mindset of continuous learning: The business world constantly evolves, and leaders must stay ahead. This means being a lifelong learner, continually seeking new knowledge and insights, and adapting your approach based on new information.

Cultivate a culture of innovation: Leaders should foster a culture that embraces experimentation, risk-taking, and the pursuit of new ideas. Encourage your team to think outside the box and challenge the status quo.

Be agile and flexible: The ability to pivot quickly and adapt to changing circumstances is crucial in today's market. Leaders must be willing to adjust their plans, make course corrections, and seize opportunities as they arise.

Focus on customer needs: The key to success in any market is understanding and meeting your customers' needs. Stay connected to your customers, gather feedback, and adapt your products and services to meet their evolving demands.

Embrace technology: Technology is a powerful tool that can be used to enhance efficiency, improve customer experience, and gain a competitive edge. Embrace new technologies and integrate them into your business processes.

Adapting to market changes isn't just about surviving; it's about thriving. Leaders who can anticipate, embrace, and leverage these shifts are the ones who will shape the future of their industries and drive lasting success.

Remember, adapting is a critical skill for any leader navigating the dynamic landscape of the digital age. It's not just about reacting to change; it's about anticipating, embracing, and shaping it to your advantage.

Balancing Vision with Execution

Balancing visionary ideas with effective execution is a hallmark of successful leaders. It's a delicate dance—holding onto a compelling vision while keeping your feet firmly planted in the reality of implementation. Imagine a leader who paints a breathtaking picture of the future, filled with innovative products, happy customers, and a thriving company. However, without a clear roadmap and the discipline to execute, that vision remains a beautiful dream, fading into the mist of unfulfilled potential.

This balancing act is particularly crucial in the rapidly evolving digital landscape. Disruptive technologies, shifting market dynamics, and a constant influx of new information demand agile leadership that can adapt, pivot, and execute with precision.

Take the example of Elon Musk, the visionary leader behind Tesla and SpaceX. His ambition is undeniable, reaching for the stars with his electric vehicles and space exploration endeavors. But his success rests on his unwavering focus on execution. He pushes his teams to constantly innovate and refine their processes, ensuring the grand vision translates into tangible results.

While visionary leaders might be naturally drawn to the excitement of new ideas, they need to cultivate a deep understanding of the practicalities of execution. This involves understanding the nuances of resource allocation, building efficient teams, and navigating the complexities of project management.

Think of it as a two-pronged approach. The first prong is about dreaming big and envisioning a future that inspires and motivates. This is the realm of creativity, where bold ideas take flight and innovative solutions are born. The second prong is about the nitty-gritty of making those dreams a reality. It's about strategic planning, meticulous implementation, and a willingness to adapt along the way.

To illustrate this point, let's consider the case of Amazon, which has successfully navigated the balancing act between vision and execution. Jeff Bezos, the founder and former CEO, envisioned a world where customers could access virtually anything they needed at the click of a button.

His vision was ambitious and transformative, but it also required a meticulous approach to execution.

Amazon's relentless focus on customer experience, operational efficiency, and technological innovation enabled them to turn their vision into a global e-commerce behemoth. They understood that while the vision was inspiring, it was the meticulous execution that ultimately drove their success.

So, how do you, as a leader, strike this balance? It's a journey of continuous learning and adaptation. Here are some key principles to guide you:

Start with a Clear Vision: Begin by articulating a clear and compelling vision that inspires your team. This vision should be both ambitious and achievable, offering a roadmap for the future. Be passionate about your vision and communicate it with enthusiasm and clarity.

Break Down the Vision into Actionable Steps: Once you have a clear vision, it's crucial to translate it into concrete action steps. Divide your goals into manageable milestones, creating a roadmap for execution.

Build a Strong and Agile Team: Surround yourself with a talented and diverse team that shares your vision and possesses the skills necessary to execute it. Encourage collaboration, open communication, and a willingness to learn from each other.

Embrace a Culture of Innovation: Foster an environment where creativity is encouraged and rewarded. Encourage your team to experiment, explore new ideas, and challenge the status quo.

Prioritize Execution: While visionary thinking is important, execution delivers results. Develop systems and processes that streamline your workflow, improve efficiency, and track progress toward your goals.

Be Adaptable and Iterative: The digital age is characterized by constant change. Be prepared to adjust your plans, learn from your mistakes, and iterate based on feedback.

Seek Feedback and Learn from Others: Listen to your team, customers, and industry experts for valuable insights. Be open to feedback and willing to adjust your approach as needed.

The path to leadership success is not a straight line. It's filled with twists, turns, and unexpected detours. Balancing vision with execution requires a leader who is both a dreamer and a doer, someone who can inspire and motivate their team while staying grounded in the reality of execution.

Just as a skilled conductor guides an orchestra through a symphony of notes, a successful leader guides their team through a complex symphony of ideas and actions. The ability to harmonize visionary thinking with the discipline of execution is what transforms a leader into a true maestro of success.

Chapter 6

Your Roadmap to Leadership Success

Crafting Your Leadership Vision

Your leadership vision is the compass that guides you and your team with a clear sense of direction through the ever-changing landscape of the digital age. It's a lofty goal and a living, breathing document that evolves with your journey. It defines what you stand for, what you aspire to achieve, and how you plan to make a difference.

Imagine a ship setting sail without a map or a destination in mind. It might be a thrilling adventure for a while, but ultimately, it will get lost and end up nowhere. Similarly, leading without a clear vision can lead to confusion, frustration, and a lack of progress.

So, how do you craft a leadership vision that is both compelling and effective? It starts with a deep understanding of yourself, your values, and your aspirations. Ask yourself:

What motivates you?

What makes you passionate about leading? What do you want to achieve? What impact do you want to make?

What are your core values?

What are the principles that guide your decisions and actions? How do these values shape your leadership style?

What is your unique contribution?

What skills, knowledge, and experiences do you bring to the table? What makes you different from other leaders?

What are your goals for the future?

What do you hope to accomplish in the next year, five or even ten years?

How can your leadership help you achieve these goals?

Once you clearly understand your core values, motivations, and goals, you can start to translate these into a written vision statement. It should be concise, compelling, and easily understood by others.

Here are some tips for crafting a powerful leadership vision:

Keep it simple and concise: Your vision should be easily remembered and communicated. Aim for a statement that is a maximum of a few sentences long.

Focus on impact: What do you want to achieve? How will your leadership contribute to a positive change in your team, organization, or the world?

Use strong language: Words have power. Use language that is evocative, inspiring, and memorable.

Be authentic: Your vision should reflect your values and your true self. Don't try to be someone you're not.

Involve your team: The best vision statements are collaborative. Encourage your team members to share their ideas and perspectives. For instance, you can conduct brainstorming sessions or one-on-one discussions to gather their input. This not only enriches your vision but also fosters a sense of ownership and commitment among your team members.

Let's say you're a product manager leading a team of developers building a new software application. Your vision could be something like:

"To empower our users with innovative technology that solves real-world problems and positively impacts society."

This vision statement is clear, concise, and impactful. It also highlights the core values of innovation, user-centricity, and social responsibility.

Remember, your leadership vision is not a static document. It should evolve as you learn, grow, and encounter new challenges. Be prepared to revisit and refine your vision as needed, ensuring it remains relevant and motivating for you and your team.

Beyond the vision statement: Once you have a clear vision, it's time to translate it into actionable steps. This involves setting specific goals and milestones that align with your overall vision.

Set SMART goals: Specific, Measurable, Achievable, Relevant, and Time-bound.

Break down significant goals into smaller steps, making them feel less daunting and more manageable.

Develop a roadmap: Outline the key milestones and deadlines for achieving your goals.

Communicate your vision and goals effectively: Regularly share your vision and goals with your team to keep everyone aligned and motivated.

Think of your leadership vision as a roadmap to success. It provides direction, clarity, and a sense of purpose. By constantly refining and adapting your vision, you can lead your team toward a brighter future, navigate the complexities of the digital age, and make a meaningful impact on the world.

Setting Goals and Milestones

Imagine you're embarking on a grand adventure, a journey to conquer the peaks of leadership success. You've packed your gear, equipped yourself with knowledge, and are ready to set off. But without a clear map and strategic checkpoints, your adventure might lead to aimless wandering. This is where setting goals and milestones comes into play.

Goals are like the towering mountains you aspire to climb, each representing a significant achievement. Milestones are the smaller peaks and passes along the way, guiding you toward your ultimate destination. They break down the journey into manageable chunks, making it feel less daunting and providing opportunities for celebration along the way.

Think of a seasoned climber who sets out to conquer Mount Everest. They don't just jump straight into the ascent. Instead, they meticulously plan their route, identifying base camps, training regimes, and acclimatization periods. These are their milestones, each one contributing to their ultimate goal.

In the realm of leadership, goals and milestones are equally crucial. Whether you're leading a team, managing a department, or steering an entire organization, having clearly defined goals and milestones provides direction, focus, and a sense of progress. They help you:

Align your efforts: When everyone on the team understands the overarching goals and the individual milestones that contribute to them, everyone's efforts become synchronized. There's a shared sense of purpose, preventing unnecessary diversions and ensuring everyone pulls in the same direction.

Measure progress: Milestones act as checkpoints, allowing you to assess your progress toward achieving your goals. This constant evaluation is crucial for staying on track, identifying potential roadblocks, and making necessary adjustments.

Celebrate achievements: Reaching a milestone is an opportunity to acknowledge and celebrate your team's hard work and dedication. It's not just a pat on the back; it's a powerful tool for boosting morale and motivating everyone to strive for greater heights. Celebrating achievements reinforces the sense of accomplishment and inspires your team to continue their journey toward the ultimate goal.

However, setting goals and milestones is not a rigid formula. It's an iterative and dynamic process that requires constant evaluation and adaptation. Here's a step-by-step approach to ensure your goals are both ambitious and achievable:

Define your vision: Start with a clear vision of where you want to lead your team or organization. This vision should be compelling, inspiring, and resonate with the values and aspirations of your team.

Set SMART goals: Once you have your vision, break it down into specific, measurable, achievable, relevant, and time-bound (SMART) goals. SMART goals provide clarity, focus, and accountability.

> **Specific**: Your goals should be clearly defined, leaving no room for ambiguity. Instead of saying, "Increase sales," be specific: "Increase sales by 15% in the next quarter."

> **Measurable**: Your goals should be quantifiable. How will you know when you've achieved them? "Increase website traffic" is less effective than "Increase website traffic by 20% within three months."

> **Achievable**: Your goals should be challenging but attainable. Set goals within reach and push your team to strive for excellence. A goal of "Increase sales by 100% overnight" is unrealistic and demotivating.

> **Relevant**: Your goals should align with your overall vision and strategy. Set goals that are relevant and focused on your core objectives.

> **Time-bound**: Set a specific timeframe for achieving your goals. Having a deadline creates a sense of urgency and encourages proactive action.

Break goals into milestones: Once you have your SMART goals, break them into smaller, more manageable ones.

These milestones are steppingstones, each contributing to the overall goal.

Assign responsibilities: Clear accountability is crucial for success. Assign specific responsibilities for achieving each milestone to individuals or teams. This ensures everyone knows their role and is accountable for their contribution.

Regularly review and adjust: The journey to leadership success is rarely linear. As you progress, you'll encounter unforeseen challenges and opportunities. Periodically review your goals and milestones, adapting them based on new information or changing circumstances.

Celebrate achievements: Reaching a milestone is a cause for celebration. Recognize and appreciate the hard work and dedication of your team. Celebrate their successes, reinforcing their commitment to the shared vision.

Remember, setting goals and milestones is not about rigid adherence to a fixed plan. It's about having a roadmap that provides direction, focus, and flexibility. It's about embracing the journey of leadership, celebrating the milestones along the way, and constantly adapting to the ever-changing landscape of the digital age.

Think of goals and milestones as the GPS navigation system for your leadership journey. They provide clear directions, help you avoid dead ends, and ensure you reach your destination. With a well-defined roadmap, you can confidently navigate the dynamic world of modern leadership, leading your team to success in the digital jungle.

Building Your Personal Leadership Brand

In today's digital world, your brand is more important than ever. It's about your skills and experience and how you present yourself as a leader. Your personal leadership brand is the perception others have of you as a leader, and it can be the key to unlocking new opportunities, influencing others, and achieving your goals.

Imagine you're a chef. You have exceptional culinary skills, but you're cooking in a dingy, uninviting kitchen with no menu. Would people flock to your establishment? Probably not. Imagine you're in a beautiful, modern restaurant with a carefully curated menu showcasing your skills; people would be drawn to your brand and eager to experience your culinary expertise.

Your personal leadership brand works similarly. It's about creating a clear, compelling, and positive image of yourself as a leader. This image is built upon your values, expertise, communication style, and overall presence.

Crafting Your Brand Foundation

The first step in building a strong personal leadership brand is understanding your core values and what makes you unique. What are your strengths? What are you passionate about? What are your professional goals? Reflecting on these questions will help you define your brand identity.

Think of your leadership style as a unique blend of ingredients. Do you focus on empowering others, leading with empathy, or driving innovation? Are you a collaborative leader, a strategic thinker, or a hands-on problem solver? Identifying these core values will help you communicate your brand effectively.

Building Your Brand Story

Once you clearly understand your core values, it's time to craft your brand story. This story should encapsulate your journey as a leader, highlighting your accomplishments, lessons learned, and aspirations.

Here are some tips for crafting a compelling brand story:

Be authentic: Don't try to be someone you're not. Be genuine and let your personality shine through.

Showcase your impact: Highlight the positive outcomes you've achieved as a leader. What tangible results have you delivered?

Embrace your challenges: Share your struggles and how you've overcome them. This demonstrates resilience and shows you're unafraid to learn from your mistakes.

Emphasize your vision: What is your vision for the future? Where do you see yourself making a difference?

Building Your Online Presence

In the digital age, your online presence is essential to your personal leadership brand. You need to create a professional and engaging presence across various online platforms.

LinkedIn: This platform is a must for any leader. Build a robust profile that showcases your expertise, achievements, and professional network. Actively engage in discussions, share insightful content, and connect with other leaders in your field.

Blog or Website: Consider starting your own blog or creating a website to share your insights, perspectives, and thought leadership. This allows you to establish yourself as an expert and build a following.

Social Media: While it's essential to maintain a professional presence on social media platforms like Twitter and Instagram, be mindful of your content. Share relevant industry news, insightful articles, and engaging stories that resonate with your audience.

Content Creation: Create valuable content that showcases your expertise and provides value to your audience. This could include articles, blog posts, videos, podcasts, or online courses.

Networking and Visibility

Building your personal leadership brand also involves networking and increasing your visibility. Attend industry events, join relevant organizations, and connect with other leaders in your field.

Building Relationships

At the heart of a strong personal leadership brand is genuine connection. Build relationships with colleagues, mentors, and peers. Be approachable, actively listen, and offer support to others.

Continuous Improvement

Like any well-crafted brand, your personal leadership brand is not static. It's an ongoing journey of continuous improvement. Seek feedback, reflect on your experiences, and constantly learn and adapt.

Ultimately, your personal leadership brand reflects who you are as a leader. It's a blend of your values, skills, experiences, and commitment to making a positive impact.

By crafting a strong personal leadership brand, you can position yourself as a sought-after leader, inspire others, and achieve your goals.

Continuous Learning and Adaptation

In the ever-evolving digital landscape, the ability to learn and adapt is no longer just a desirable trait for leaders; it's necessary. The business world is constantly in flux, driven by technological advancements, shifting consumer preferences, and global events. Leaders who cling to outdated methods and resist change will be left behind.

Think of a seasoned sailor navigating uncharted waters. They can't rely solely on the maps of the past; they need to constantly observe, adjust their course, and embrace new tools. This is the mindset that successful leaders adopt. It's not just about acquiring knowledge but about developing the agility to apply it in real-time, responding to unexpected challenges and opportunities.

Here are some key principles for continuous learning and adaptation in leadership:

Cultivate a Growth Mindset: At its core, continuous learning is about embracing a growth mindset. This mindset recognizes that knowledge and skills are not fixed but can be developed through effort and experience. Leaders with a growth mindset are perpetually seeking feedback, challenging their assumptions, and pushing their boundaries. They view failures as learning opportunities, not setbacks.

Embrace the Power of Technology: The digital age has democratized access to information, making learning more accessible than ever before. Online courses, webinars, and digital platforms offer a vast library of resources for leaders to expand their knowledge base. From mastering the latest project management software to understanding the intricacies of artificial intelligence, embracing technology is key to staying relevant.

Seek Diverse Perspectives: One of the most effective ways to learn and adapt is to expose yourself to diverse perspectives. Connect with individuals from different backgrounds, industries, and areas of expertise. Attend industry conferences, engage in cross-functional collaborations, and actively seek out dissenting opinions. You challenge your assumptions and broaden your understanding of the world by stepping outside your comfort zone.

Embrace Experimentation and Innovation: Successful leaders are fearless and take calculated risks. They encourage a culture of innovation where new ideas are welcomed and tested. Even if it leads to setbacks, experimentation provides valuable data points that inform future decision-making. The key is to create a safe space for experimentation, fostering a culture where learning from mistakes is valued.

Practice Active Listening and Feedback: Learning doesn't happen in isolation. Leaders must be active listeners, seeking and valuing feedback from their teams, stakeholders, and competitors. This feedback provides valuable insights into what's working, what's not, and where adjustments are needed. It's a continuous cycle of learning, adapting, and improving.

Seek Mentorship and Coaching: Mentorship and coaching are invaluable tools for leadership development. A trusted advisor to guide you through challenges, provide objective feedback, and offer strategic guidance can accelerate your learning curve. Find mentors with experience in areas where you need to grow, and seek out coaches who can help you develop specific skills.

Embrace the Power of Storytelling: Effective communication is critical to leadership. Leaders who can effectively convey their vision, inspire their teams, and articulate their strategy through compelling stories are likelier to succeed. Learning to craft stories that resonate with audiences, building emotional connections, and sharing experiences can enhance your leadership impact.

Continuous Learning in Action: Real-World Examples

To illustrate these principles, let's look at some real-world examples of how leaders have embraced constant learning and adaptation:

Elon Musk at Tesla: Musk is a prime example of a leader who continuously pushes the boundaries of innovation. He is obsessed with learning, constantly seeking new technologies and challenging the status quo. His relentless pursuit of knowledge and willingness to adapt has led to the creation of groundbreaking electric vehicles and advancements in renewable energy.

Satya Nadella at Microsoft: Nadella took over a Microsoft that was struggling to adapt to the rise of cloud computing. He recognized the need for a significant cultural shift, focusing on agility, collaboration, and innovation. Under

Nadella's leadership, Microsoft transformed itself into a leader in the cloud space, demonstrating the power of embracing change and continuous learning.

Indra Nooyi at PepsiCo: Nooyi's leadership at PepsiCo was marked by a commitment to diversity, inclusivity, and sustainability. She recognized the importance of fostering a culture of learning and adaptation, encouraging her team to embrace new ideas and challenge conventional thinking. Nooyi's focus on continuous learning and innovation helped PepsiCo navigate a rapidly changing consumer landscape.

These examples showcase how embracing continuous learning and adaptation is not just a strategy for individual success; it's a key driver of organizational success. Leaders who prioritize learning, embrace technology, seek diverse perspectives, and cultivate a culture of innovation are better equipped to navigate the challenges and opportunities of the 21st century.

Leading with Purpose and Passion

Leadership is not just about titles or authority; it's about inspiring and empowering others to reach their full potential.

It's about creating a shared vision and guiding your team toward a common goal. However, authentic leadership, the kind that leaves a lasting impact, is rooted in purpose and passion. This fuel drives you, keeps you motivated, and allows you to connect with your team.

Imagine a ship captain navigating stormy seas. Without a clear destination, the journey becomes aimless, and the crew loses motivation. But when the captain has a purpose – to reach a specific port, to deliver vital cargo, or to explore new horizons –

the crew rallies behind them. They understand the importance of their collective effort, and their passion ignites. This purpose-driven leadership keeps the ship on course and empowers the crew to overcome challenges and achieve remarkable things.

In the digital age, where change is constant, and innovation is the norm, it's more important than ever for leaders to have a strong sense of purpose. This purpose doesn't have to be grand or world-changing; it can be as simple as positively impacting your team, improving a process, or creating a product that makes people's lives easier. What matters is that your purpose is genuine, significant to you, and aligns with your values.

Think of the leaders who have inspired you. Were they driven by a desire for personal gain or a larger vision, a belief in something greater than themselves? Most likely, they were fueled by a passion for making a difference.

Whether it's Elon Musk's ambition to revolutionize transportation or Marie Curie's dedication to scientific discovery, these leaders are driven by a deep-seated passion that inspires others to follow their lead.

Passion is contagious. When you're genuinely passionate about your work, it's impossible to hide it. Your enthusiasm and energy are infectious, and they inspire those around you.

A passionate leader can turn an ordinary team into a high-performing one simply by igniting the spark of passion in their team members.

How do you cultivate this vital combination of purpose and passion?

Reflect on Your Values: Take some time for introspection. What are your core values? What drives you? What are you passionate about? Perhaps it's a desire to create innovative solutions, to empower others, or to make a positive impact on the world. Once you clearly understand your values, you can align your goals and actions with them.

Discover Your Why: Ask yourself: Why am I doing this? What is the bigger picture? Is it to build a successful company, to improve the lives of others, to leave a lasting legacy? Identifying your "why" gives you a sense of purpose and helps you stay motivated through challenging times.

Connect With Your Passion: What excites you? What are you naturally drawn to? It could be problem-solving, creative thinking, or building relationships. Find ways to incorporate these passions into your work. When you do what you love, your passion will shine through, inspiring your team and creating a more fulfilling work environment.

Share Your Vision: Once you have a clear vision and purpose, communicate it to your team. Inspire them with your passion and enthusiasm. Paint a compelling picture of the future you are striving for. When your team understands your "why" and shares your vision, they are more likely to be engaged, committed, and motivated.

Celebrate Milestones: Celebrating achievements and acknowledging your team's contributions is essential. This reinforces their sense of purpose and keeps them motivated. Recognizing milestones also creates a sense of accomplishment and builds a positive team culture.

Embrace Continuous Learning: The world is constantly changing, and so are the challenges we face as leaders. Embrace a growth mindset and be open to continuous learning. Seek new knowledge, explore different perspectives, and adapt your leadership style. By continuously expanding your knowledge and skills, you stay relevant and inspire your team to do the same.

Lead by Example: Your actions speak louder than words. Be the change you want to see in your team. Demonstrate the values you believe in, embody the passion you want to cultivate and set an example for others to follow. Your team will mirror your behavior, and your leadership will ripple throughout the organization.

Leading with purpose and passion is not a destination but a journey. It's an ongoing commitment to self-reflection, growth, and the continuous pursuit of meaningful work.

When you align your actions with your core values and inspire your team with your vision and passion, you create a truly impactful leadership style that leaves a lasting legacy.

Remember, leadership is not about power but the power to influence and inspire others to achieve greatness.

So, embrace your purpose, ignite your passion, and lead wholeheartedly.

Glossary of Terms

This glossary defines key terms used throughout the book:

Agile: A methodology emphasizing iterative development, collaboration, and customer feedback.

Artificial Intelligence (AI): The ability of machines to perform tasks that typically require human intelligence.

Cloud Computing: The delivery of computing services—including servers, storage, databases, networking, software, analytics, and intelligence—over the internet ("the cloud").

Emotional Intelligence (EQ): The ability to perceive, understand, manage, and use emotions.

Growth Mindset: A belief that abilities and intelligence can be developed through effort and learning.

Remote Work: Working from a location other than a traditional office, such as home or a co-working space.

Resilience: The ability to adapt and bounce back from adversity.

Team Culture: The shared values, beliefs, and behaviors that characterize a team.

Acknowledgments

This book wouldn't be possible without the contributions of many incredible individuals. First and foremost, I want to thank my family and friends for their unwavering support and encouragement throughout this journey. Your belief in me has been a constant source of inspiration.

I am deeply grateful to the industry leaders and experts who shared their insights and stories. Your experiences and wisdom have enriched this book and provided invaluable lessons for readers.

Finally, I want to thank all the readers who are about to embark on this journey with me. I hope this book empowers you to embrace the challenges and opportunities of modern leadership.

Notes

Chapter 1 – Rethinking Leadership

LinkedIn "Why Command & Control Leadership doesn't work, and what to do instead" (https://www.linkedin.com/pulse/why-command-control-leadership-doesnt-work-what-do-instead-wheatley/)

Forbes "You Can Control, And You Can Lead, But You Can't Do Both" (https://www.forbes.com/sites/forbescoachescouncil/2018/07/25/you-can-control-and-you-can-lead-but-you-cant-do-both/)

Forbes "How Tesla is Revolutionizing Management to Save The Planet" (https://www.forbes.com/sites/stevedenning/2023/07/05/how-tesla-is-revolutionizing-management-to-save-the-planet/)

Business Chief "Tesla's Innovation Culture: How Elon Musk Drives Excellence" (https://businesschief.com/articles/teslas-innovation-culture-how-elon-musk-drives-creative-ex)

GoTech Career. "Insights Into Netflix Work Culture And What to Expect." (https://gotechcareer.com/insights-into-netflix-work-culture-and-what-to-expect/)

Life at Spotify. "Work isn't somewhere you go, it's something you do" (https://www.lifeatspotify.com/being-here/work-from-anywhere)

Harvard Business Review. "GitLab's CEO on Building One of the World's Largest All-Remote Companies". (https://hbr.org/2023/03/gitlabs-ceo-on-building-one-of-the-worlds-largest-all-remote-companies)

Forbes "Elon Musk: A Visionary Entrepreneur Shaping the Future" (https://forbes.com.ph/billionaires/elon-musk-a-visionary-entrepreneur-shaping-the-future/)

Charles Darwin *It's not the strongest of the species that survives, nor the most intelligent, but the one most adaptable to change"* - The Origin of Species"24-Nov-1859

GoTech Career. "Insights Into Netflix Work Culture And What to Expect." (https://gotechcareer.com/insights-into-netflix-work-culture-and-what-to-expect/)

Digitopia. "Netflix Culture: Fostering Innovation Through Freedom and Responsibility." (https://digitopia.co/blog/netflix-culture/)

Braden Kelley. "How Netflix Built a Culture of Innovation." (https://bradenkelley.com/2021/08/how-netflix-built-a-culture-of-innovation/)

CultureMonkey. "Netflix's Company Culture: The Unconventional Approach That Shattered Corporate Norms." (https://www.culturemonkey.io/employee-engagement/netflix-culture/)

Harvard Business School. "Netflix: A Creative Approach to Culture and Agility." (https://www.hbs.edu/faculty/Pages/item.aspx?num=56185)

Geeknack. "Google Leadership Principles At a Glance" (https://www.geeknack.com/2020/07/31/google-leadership-principles-at-a-glance/)

Strategos. "How Google Manages Continuous Innovation in a Rapidly Changing World" (https://strategos.com/google-model-managing-continuous-innovation-rapidly-changing-world/)

Chapter 2 – Navigating Remote Work

Harvard Business Review. "GitLab's CEO on Building One of the World's Largest All-Remote Companies". (https://hbr.org/2023/03/gitlabs-ceo-on-building-one-of-the-worlds-largest-all-remote-companies)

Zapier "The Remote Work Report by Zapier" (https://zapier.com/blog/remote-work-report-by-zapier/?msockid=0a2c5f85f54a60a63c6e4ab7f4256129)

Forbes "Whatever The CEO Says, Hybrid Working Is Here To Stay" (https://www.forbes.com/councils/forbesbusinesscouncil/2024/02/26/whatever-the-ceo-says-hybrid-working-is-here-to-stay/)

Digitopia. "Netflix Culture: Fostering Innovation Through Freedom and Responsibility." (https://digitopia.co/blog/netflix-culture/)

Braden Kelley. "How Netflix Built a Culture of Innovation." (https://bradenkelley.com/2021/08/how-netflix-built-a-culture-of-innovation/)

CultureMonkey. "Netflix's Company Culture: The Unconventional Approach That Shattered Corporate Norms."

(https://www.culturemonkey.io/employee-engagement/netflix-culture/)

Harvard Business School. "Netflix: A Creative Approach to Culture and Agility." (https://www.hbs.edu/faculty/Pages/item.aspx?num=56185)

Microsoft. "Microsoft's Sr Leaders Bring Employees Together in COVID-19." (https://www.microsoft.com/insidetrack/blog/microsofts-senior-leaders-bring-employees-together-during-covid-19/)

Microsoft. "Satya Nadella Talks to Adam Grant About the Future of Work." (https://www.microsoft.com/en-us/worklab/satya-nadella-talks-to-adam-grant-about-the-future-of-work)

Nasdaq. "Here's What Satya Nadella Is Telling Microsoft Employees About COVID-19." (https://www.nasdaq.com/articles/heres-what-satya-nadella-is-telling-microsoft-employees-about-covid-19-2020-03-24)

LinkedIn "Buffer's Path to Success: Cultivating a Remote Work Culture of Transparency and Well-being" (https://www.linkedin.com/pulse/buffers-path-success-cultivating-remote-work-6hcde/)

Buffer "2022 State Of Remote Work" (https://buffer.com/state-of-remote-work/2022)

The Git Hub Blog "Remote work: A series of best practices for a remote workplace" (https://github.blog/news-insights/remote-work-a-series-of-best-practices-for-a-remote-workplace/)

Chapter 3 – Building Resilient Teams

Atlassian. "Discover the Spotify model: What the most popular music technology company can teach us about scaling agile" (https://www.atlassian.com/agile/agile-at-scale/spotify#:~:text=The%20Spotify%20model%20is%20a%20people-driven%2C%20autonomous%20approach,by%20focusing%20on%20autonomy%2C%20communication%2C%20accountability%2C%20and%20quality.)

Forbes "How Airbnb Survived The Pandemic – And How You Can Too" (https://www.forbes.com/sites/deniselyohn/2020/11/10/how-airbnb-survived-the-pandemic--and-how-you-can-too/)

Science of Mind "Unlocking Motivation: How Does Google Motivate Their Employees" (https://scienceofmind.org/how-does-google-motivate-their-employees/)

CNBC "Jeff Bezos on learning from failure: 'Whatever your goals are, don't give up no matter how hard it gets" (https://www.cnbc.com/2021/10/03/jeff-bezos-on-failure-dont-give-up-no-matter-how-hard-it-gets.html?msockid=0a2c5f85f54a60a63c6e4ab7f4256129)

Microsoft. "Satya Nadella on Leading Through Change: Building a Culture of Innovation." (https://www.microsoft.com/en-us/worklab/satya-nadella-talks-to-adam-grant-about-the-future-of-work)

Sheryl Sandberg. "Lean In: Women, Work, and the Will to Lead." (https://leanin.org/book)

Geeknack. "Sheryl Sandberg Leadership Style & Principles." (https://www.geeknack.com/2020/10/10/sheryl-sandberg-leadership-style-principles/)

Ventures Digest. "Sheryl Sandberg's Leadership Style: A Case Study in Corporate Success." (https://venturesdigest.com/sheryl-sandbergs-leadership-style-a-case-study-in-corporate-success/)

LeanIn. "Leadership Lessons with Shellye Archambeau & Sheryl Sandberg." (https://leanin.org/tilted-podcast-season-2/leadership)

Science Alert "Here's How SpaceX Went From 3 Failed Launches to Sending Humans Into Space" (https://www.sciencealert.com/here-s-the-story-of-how-spacex-got-to-this-incredible-moment-in-space-exploration)

Fox Sports "Flashback: Red Sox end Curse of the Bambino in 2004 World Series" (https://www.foxsports.com/stories/mlb/flashback-red-sox-end-curse-of-the-bambino-in-2004-world-series)

Reader's Digest "33 Miners, Buried Alive for 69 Days: This Is Their Remarkable Survival Story" (https://www.rd.com/article/chilean-miners-buried-alive/)

Chapter 4 – Nurturing Creativity and Innovation

Forbes "Is Elon Musk The Greatest Leader On Earth?" (https://www.forbes.com/sites/sallypercy/2023/09/26/is-elon-musk-the-greatest-leader-on-earth/)

The World Financial Review "Elon Musk — An Inspirational Icon for Generation X Globally" (https://worldfinancialreview.com/elon-musk-%e2%80%95-an-inspirational-icon-for-generation-x-globally/)

CNBC "Google's "20% Rule" shows exactly how much time you should spend learning new skills – and why it works" (https://www.cnbc.com/2021/12/16/google-20-percent-rule-shows-exactly-how-much-time-you-should-spend-learning-new-skills.html#:~:text=Enter%3A%20Google%27s%20%2220%25%20time%22%20rule%2C%20a%20concept%20made,and%20Larry%20Page%20wrote%20in%20their%20IPO%20letter.?msockid=0a2c5f85f54a60a63c6e4ab7f4256129)

Shortform "The Netflix Freedom and Responsibility Culture" (https://www.shortform.com/blog/netflix-freedom-and-respon-sibility/)

Great Learning "Tesla's Design Thinking Approach: How Design Thinking worked for Tesla" (https://www.mygreatlearning.com/blog/teslas-design-thinking-approach-how-design-thinking-worked-for-tesla/#The%20real%20ap-proach%20of%20Tesla%20towards%20design%20thinking)

Forbes "Tesla: A History Of Innovation (and Headaches)" (https://www.forbes.com/sites/qai/2022/09/29/tesla-a-history-of-innovation-and-headaches/)

Medium "How Airbnb used design thinking, innovation, and creativity to overcome early challenges" (https://medium.com/@pardhi.mbahr03/how-airbnb-used-de-sign-thinking-innovation-and-creativity-to-overcome-early-challenges-48f40ffa0052)

Great Learning "Tesla's Design Thinking Approach: How Design Thinking worked for Tesla" (https://www.mygreatlearning.com/

blog/teslas-design-thinking-approach-how-design-thinking-worked-for-tesla/#The%20real%20ap-proach%20of%20Tesla%20towards%20design%20thinking)

Forbes "Tesla: A History Of Innovation (and Headaches)" (https://www.forbes.com/sites/qai/2022/09/29/tesla-a-history-of-innovation-and-headaches/)

Harvard Business School. "Netflix: A Creative Approach to Culture and Agility." (https://www.hbs.edu/faculty/Pages/item.aspx?num=56185)

Strategos. "How Google Manages Continuous Innovation in a Rapidly Changing World" (https://strategos.com/google-model-managing-continuous-innovation-rapidly-changing-world/)

CNBC "Google's "20% Rule" shows exactly how much time you should spend learning new skills – and why it works" (https://www.cnbc.com/2021/12/16/google-20-percent-rule-shows-exactly-how-much-time-you-should-spend-learning-new-skills.html#:~:text=Enter%3A%20Google%27s%20%2220%25%20time%22%20rule%2C%20a%20concept%20made,and%20Larry%20Page%20wrote%20in%20their%20IPO%20letter.?msockid=0a2c5f85f54a60a63c6e4ab7f4256129)

CNBC "How Google parent Alphabet invests in start-ups" https://www.cnbc.com/2017/08/17/alphabet-google-start-up-investment-vehi-cles.html?msockid=0a2c5f85f54a60a63c6e4ab7f4256129)

Chapter 5 – Insights From Industry Leaders

DZone "Research Beats Best Practices: A Google Leadership Thought Process" (https://dzone.com/articles/research-beats-best-practices-a-google-leadership)

Harvard Business Review "How Apple Is Organized for Innovation" (https://hbr.org/2020/11/how-apple-is-organized-for-innovation)

Forbes "Elon Musk: A Visionary Entrepreneur Shaping the Future" (https://forbes.com.ph/billionaires/elon-musk-a-visionary-entrepreneur-shaping-the-future/)

Builtin "7 Leadership Lessons From Netflix Co-Founder Reed Hastings" (https://builtin.com/company-culture/netflix-book)

LinkedIn "Inside Airbnb: Reflecting on Brian Chesky's Visionary Approach to Leadership, Growth, and Innovation" (https://www.linkedin.com/pulse/inside-airbnb-reflecting-brian-cheskys-visionary-approach-paul-hyman-unrre/)

Pressfarm "Leadership Lessons from Airbnb CEO Brian Chesky" (https://press.farm/leadership-lessons-airbnb-ceo-brian-chesky/)

Fast Company "Snap is the World's Most Innovative Company of 2020" (https://www.fastcompany.com/90457684/snap-most-innovative-companies-2020)

Pressfarm. "Elon Musk's Autodidactic Approach: A Model for Lifelong Learning" (https://press.farm/elon-musks-autodidactic-approach-to-learning/)

Pressfarm. "Elon Musk's Mentors: Influential Figures in His Educational Path" (https://press.farm/elon-musks-mentors-and-influential-figures/)

Forbes "PepsiCo's Indra Nooyi, The Queen Of Pop, Shares Her Tips For Bringing Compassionate Leadership To Work" (https://www.forbes.com/sites/janehanson/2022/04/30/pepsicos-indra-nooyi-the-queen-of-pop-shares-her-tips-for-bringing-compassionate-leadership-to-work/?sh=74b5df467cb1)

Conferences for Women "Leadership Lessons with Trailblazer Indra Nooyi" (https://www.conferencesforwomen.org/leadership-lessons-indra-nooyi/)

LinkedIn "The Titans of Entrepreneurship Series: Indra Nooyi" (https://www.linkedin.com/pulse/titans-entrepreneurship-series-indra-nooyi-zafar-khan/)

Pressfarm "Satya Nadella and Bill Gates: Collaboration of Microsoft's Leaders" (https://press.farm/satya-nadella-and-bill-gates-collaboration/)

Economic Times "Microsoft CEO Satya Nadella: 10 interesting facts" (https://economictimes.indiatimes.com/people/microsoft-ceo-satya-nadella-10-interesting-facts/born-in-hyderabad/slideshow/52395811.cms)

BBC "Netflix's history: From DVD rentals to streaming success" (https://www.bbc.com/news/newsbeat-42788099)

BBC "Amazon at 25: The story of a giant" (https://www.bbc.com/news/business-48884596)

Forbes "Amazon At 25: A Fascinating Journey Through Retail History" (https://www.forbes.com/sites/neilstern/2019/07/11/amazon-at-25-a-fascinating-journey-through-retail-history/)

The New York Times "Patagonia's Profits Are Funding Conservation — and Politics" (https://www.nytimes.com/2024/01/30/climate/patagonia-holdfast-philanthropy.html)

McKinsey & Company "Patagonia shows how turning a profit doesn't have to cost the Earth" (https://www.mckinsey.com/industries/agriculture/our-insights/patagonia-shows-how-turning-a-profit-doesnt-have-to-cost-the-earth)

Harvard Business Review "Does Elon Musk Have a Strategy?" (https://hbr.org/2022/07/does-elon-musk-have-a-strategy)

Forbes "Is Elon Musk The Greatest Leader On Earth?" (https://www.forbes.com/sites/sallypercy/2023/09/26/is-elon-musk-the-greatest-leader-on-earth/)

Digitopia "Amazon's Customer Obsession: The Cultural Code Driving Unstoppable Growth" (https://digitopia.co/blog/amazons-customer-obsession/)

Medium ""Customer obsession" is key to Amazon's success" (https://medium.com/purposeful-retail/customer-obsession-is-key-to-amazons-success-4d01e062fd72)

Chapter 6 – Your Roadmap to Leadership Success

Pressfarm. "Elon Musk's Autodidactic Approach: A Model for Lifelong Learning" (https://press.farm/elon-musks-autodidactic-approach-to-learning/)

Pressfarm. "Elon Musk's Mentors: Influential Figures in His Educational Path" (https://press.farm/elon-musks-mentors-and-influential-figures/)

Harvard Business Review "How Microsoft Became Innovative Again" (https://hbr.org/2023/02/how-microsoft-became-innovative-again)

Harvard Business Review "Indra Nooyi, Former CEO of PepsiCo, on Nurturing Talent in Turbulent Times" (https://hbr.org/2021/11/indra-nooyi-former-ceo-of-pepsico-on-nurturing-talent-in-turbulent-times)

LinkedIn "Lessons from Indra Nooyi: Leadership, Innovation, and Diversity in Business" (https://www.linkedin.com/pulse/lessons-from-indra-nooyi-leadership-innovation-diversity-paria-ic8nc/)

Kari Leighton is a seasoned leader with over two decades of experience in operations management, strategic planning, and organizational transformation. Having held strategic leadership roles in industries ranging from healthcare to security services, Kari has a proven track record of driving innovation, fostering collaboration, and delivering measurable results in complex environments.

A champion of change management and a lifelong learner, Kari is passionate about empowering others to lead with agility, creativity, and emotional intelligence. Drawing from real-world experience and insights from industry pioneers, her debut book *Ctrl+Alt+Lead* is a dynamic guide to mastering leadership in the digital age.

When not strategizing or mentoring future leaders, Kari enjoys exploring the intersection of technology and human connection, bringing her vision of resilient and innovative teams to life.

www.ingramcontent.com/pod-product-compliance
Lightning Source LLC
Chambersburg PA
CBHW061526050726
47593CB00002B/679